Little Sisters

Also by Carolyn Lieberg

Calling the Midwest Home:
A Lively Look at the Origins, Attitudes, Quirks,
and Curiosities of America's Heartlanders
(Wildcat Canyon Press, 1996)

Little Sisters

The Last But Not the Least

CAROLYN LIEBERG

Wildcat Canyon Press
A Division of Circulus Publishing Group, Inc.
Berkeley, California

Little Sisters: The Last But Not the Least
Copyright © 1998 by Carolyn Lieberg
Cover photograph by Michele Clement, San Francisco

Publisher: Julienne Bennett
Editor: Roy M. Carlisle
Copyeditor: Karyn S. DiCastri
Cover and Interior Design: Gordon Chun Design
Typesetting: Holly A. Taines
Typographic Specifications: Body text set in 11.5/16 Bembo. Catull Regular is used for display.

Printed in the United States of America
Library of Congress Cataloging-in-Publication Data
Lieberg, Carolyn S.
    Little sisters : the last but not the least / Carolyn Lieberg.
       p. cm.
    Includes bibliographical references.
    ISBN 1-885171-24-2 (pbk. : alk. paper)
    1. Sisters. 2. Youngest child. 3. Sibling rivalry. I. Title.
HQ759.96.L54   1998
306.875'4—dc21   98-29819 CIP

Distributed to the trade by Publishers Group West
10 9 8 7 6 5 4 3 2 1

To Craig, every day.

And to my parents and my brother,
without whom I wouldn't have been
a little sister.

Contents

CHAPTER FOUR

Learning the Ropes and Making Our Way ✺ 147

In our early years, we learn a lot about the many uses of mischief from our siblings. Sometimes in our teens, and often in adulthood, we adopt rebellious ways for a number of reasons.

CHAPTER FIVE

Getting on with Things ✺ 175

Being a little sister influences us as adults in the workplace and at home. The lessons we learned in childhood often affect whom we are attracted to and how we behave as parents.

Introduction

Being a little sister means we're last and we're little. *Last* always, and *little* for quite a while. After years and years, we look as big and mature as other people; however, we always carry with us our history of growing up as a little sister.

When we're young, it can take quite a while to discover that we have a friend or two who are also little sisters. What a relief—another last kid with a big brother or big sister or both, someone who understands what life is like for us. We didn't stop to imagine that the world is in fact filled with little sisters, and that lots of them were having many of the same experiences we were. The truth is there are millions of little sisters—31,200,000, or so, just in the U.S. Those of us who have felt as though we belonged to a small minority can rejoice in the fact that we belong to a *huge* minority.

The little sisters who spoke to me for this book revealed many similar complaints and privileges. Apparently many of us little sisters—depending upon the ages and sexes of our older siblings—have some stories that are remarkably alike. There's comfort in finding that others had experiences that are familiar to us. And there's reassurance in hearing how we little sisters land on our feet again and again. We are a group of women who are determined and cooperative; in addition, we can be rebellious and good negotiators, to name a few of our assets.

Writing this book led me to realize how much I shared with other little sisters. Regardless of the particular obstacles that many of us faced at one time or another, it seems that most little sisters thrive on getting a fresh understanding of some of the whys of our childhood, and we come out realizing how valuable and special our pasts can be to us.

CHAPTER ONE

What's It All About?

I always wanted to be somebody,
but I should have been more specific.

– LILY TOMLIN –

Little Sisters. Who do we think we are, anyway?

To begin with, we're not alone. Now we know there are millions of little sisters in the world. This fact we may forget sometimes, because when each of us thinks about "little sister," our first image is of ourselves, of course. In each of our families, there was only one last kid, and she was us.

Being last is only part of the story, since there is wide variety in our lastness: Some little sisters have brothers, some have sisters, and some have both. Some of these older siblings are barely a year older than us, while others are several years older. These variations often influence the kinds of experiences that little sisters have. But being the final child was the destiny for each of us and, regardless of what occurs in our lives, one of the facts of life that we carry forever is that we will always be the last child in our own family—the little sister.

Finding Our Way

We little sisters—like everyone else—
have had to carve our path in the world.

❧

Whether we were taunted and teased or spoiled and cherished, whether we hated being a little sister or absolutely loved it, we little sisters—like everyone else—have had to carve our path in the world. Most of us are fairly certain that being a little sister played a big part in how we developed and still influences some aspects of how we behave. Regardless of other aspects of our identity, one section of it—larger for some than for others—is the label "little sister."

No matter how old we get or how far away we grow from our roots or from other family members, being a little sister is a characteristic that can influence and shape what we do in our love relationships, our friendships, our parenting, our decisions about jobs or recreation—perhaps even which car we buy or how we wear our hair.

In sorting through our experiences to discover how

little sisterhood has helped determine our identity, we run into lots of questions. Some of the questions are wide and general such as: Does being a little sister affect the kind of friend I am or the ways I behave as a parent? Some of the questions are specific and personal. One of my lingering questions, for instance, has always been: Why did my brother always get the largest bedroom? (Not that I had *bad* bedrooms, except maybe for that converted closet. . . .)

Even if answers to some of our questions remain elusive, the search for answers goes on. And it seems that little sisters are generally reconciled to living with some unsolved mysteries. The little sisters I spoke with were content with many aspects of their lives. Some of them had no complaints at all—a claim that many of our older siblings would envy—and the rest felt that they had overcome obstacles, made progress on dilemmas, or figured out how to live with the knotty relationships left over from their beginnings as little sisters. Many women basked in the benefits of little sisterhood, and others made good use of the attributes that little sisterhood had bestowed upon them.

The topics that affect little sisters—from the early mischievous behaviors and rivalries we feel with older siblings to the strengths that many of us discover in adulthood—all somehow contribute to our continually changing sense of who we are.

Scoundrels and Heroes

For most of us, being little meant putting up with various disadvantages as well as enjoying some sweet benefits.

❧

I found most little sisters eager and cheerfully willing to engage in reflection about their pasts. All kinds of memories surfaced—some warm, some amusing, and some still irksome. Most of us can recall childhood experiences and events that seem to have structured the family ties of our adulthood. For the most part, little sisters who are adults have put their childhood experiences into perspective; however, I also spoke with a number of women who are still trying to modify relationships with their siblings. These adult relationships can't be altered by reminiscing about nostalgia; instead, we have to focus on the dynamics we continue to experience with our adult siblings. We little sisters want to move away from some of the childish treatment we received; we want to be viewed and respected on adult terms. Even with such a serious goal in mind, both types of little sisters—those who are working to change relationships and those who enjoy mature, satisfying relationships—were happy to recount funny or touching tales from their childhoods and to describe how life was for them.

For most of us, being little meant putting up with various disadvantages as well as enjoying some sweet benefits. One way to explore how being a little sister has shaped us is to recount and compare some of our childhood memories—both the great kindnesses bestowed upon us by our older siblings and (let's admit it) some moments of conniving meanness, when our older siblings, overcome by jealousy or a simple lust for power, tricked, teased, or pained us in some way. It seems that no matter how many years pass between such kind or careless acts and the present time, little sisters get a kick out of retelling these events. Sometimes a bit of the old whine comes through, but often little sisters recall odd little tales that clearly carry some nostalgia.

Christina recalls, "My brother was my hero. He had a wonderful sense of humor, and seemed to take great pride in making me laugh. I remember him strapping my friend Kaye and I into the back of a golf cart, where the bags would go, and driving us around a local golf course, telling us jokes and talking silly. We were laughing so hard as he was saying nonsensical stuff like, 'I don't know what is wrong with you girls—I buy you books and buy you books and all you do is eat the covers!' We just thought that was hysterical. Don't ask me why!"

We little sisters often made darn good audiences.

The Littleness of Little

*Over and over again, we heard that we were
the little sister.*

❧

To return to our earliest years, imagine how bewildered we must have been by the hustle and bustle around us. All the chatter and movement. What was it about? Us. Arriving home from the hospital. Being introduced. Over and over again, we heard that we were *the little sister*.

And that is our universal title: Little Sisters. Especially Little. Consider the word itself. Little: as small. Little: as unimportant. Little: as secondary. And okay, Little: as precious. We little sisters eventually grow in stature and weight and years enough to leave the notion of smallness behind, but that growth takes a long time—a decade and a half at least, if we're lucky. And even after we've escaped the initial tininess and vulnerability of our childhoods, we slowly come to understand and realize that little isn't going to go away. Not all the way. Not ever. Not really.

For one thing, some of us stay short, which is a child-like thing to be. It doesn't help. But beyond size, this potent word, *little*, with all of its endearing and diminishing connotations, hangs around our necks with the tenacity of that dead albatross in Samuel Taylor Coleridge's poem, "The Rime of the Ancient Mariner." Its odor fades occasionally, but the shadow of it is always there to a greater or lesser extent. (And, yes, it's true we might sometimes be called "younger" or "youngest sisters," but most of the time it's "little.")

In our jobs, the littleness dissolves into the background. We run meetings, manage personnel, teach others, make decisions, create beautiful or innovative objects, and generally behave like we're in charge and, if not all-knowing, at least a bit wise. Then we go home for a holiday and ZAP! We're little sisters again. Little, lesser, minor. *Go ahead. Put me on the porch at the card table with the other little kids for Thanksgiving dinner. I know my place.* Yes, yes, we sigh. We're little sisters. That's the truth of it, for good and for ill.

Little Can Be Great

Besides finding common bonds with each other, little sisters often enjoy plenty of advantages within their families.

❧

I wonder sometimes if the peculiarities of growing up as little sisters gave us a sixth sense of some sort. It's true in my own case, and I've heard other adult little sisters describe this situation, too. When we feel an immediate connection with a new acquaintance, we often discover that the woman is a little sister. It seems that our past experiences lead us more quickly into closeness, trust, and understanding. Perhaps the cultures of our development have been similar enough to give us some common ways of living in the world, of interacting with people, of holding expectations, and of working on our goals and ambitions.

Besides finding common bonds with each other, little sisters often enjoy plenty of advantages within their families. One particular type of little sister which is nearly assured of having a blissful view of life is those last daughters who have a large age gap between themselves and their older siblings. Most of these little sisters feel that life itself was served on a silver platter. These girls, arriving eight, thirteen, or sixteen years later than the previous child are labeled "caboose babies" in scholarly literature, because of course, they trail behind. (The name cutely underscores the "lastness" of their position; I wonder what the birth order was of the person who coined the title.)

One woman who enjoyed such advantages was Peggy, the youngest of six. "I was treated very well by my two oldest sisters. They were always acting as if I was their little girl, especially the oldest and her husband. Since my sister is eighteen years older, people who didn't know my parents would always mistake her and her husband for my mom and dad." Peggy's parents were forty-one and forty-seven when she was born. "I got out of a lot of punishment," she said, "because Mom and Dad were tired from having gone through that five times previously."

Like Peggy, I had some benefits from that relationship, too, although my brother is only about four years older than I am. In fact, I experienced a big benefit: He saved my life. We were visiting my grandparents' farm, and cousin Linda, brother Jerry, and I went to the barn to get some water. Jerry and Linda were both seven and I was three. It was winter, I guess, because I had a head scarf on, tied beneath my chin.

One of the big kids turned on the motor that pumped the water. The wheel started spinning, and the rubber belt began whirling between the motor and the pump. I leaned in to watch the water spurt into the bucket and, before I knew it, the spinning belt caught a loose corner of my scarf. I must have yelled as I tugged back, but it pulled me in tighter and tighter, pressing my forehead to the racing belt. The later prediction was that the scarf would have slipped down to my neck and strangled me, but in the panic of the moment, Jerry showed presence of mind: He leaned over and turned off the switch.

My brother received high praise for his heroism, and he deserved it. The story is told occasionally when the family gathers, and sometimes Jerry takes some pleasure in teasing me about missing his chance to return to only-child status. Ho Ho.

There's no question that we little sisters are often lucky to be under the care of our big brothers and sisters. They tug us from swimming pools and jerk us out of the way of speeding bicycles. They fix our toys and show us how to tie a square knot. Despite their capacity for being as mischievous as they can be, we all know they can be sweethearts to us, too.

Making It Big

It's no surprise that lots of women who are little sisters have made an impact on culture.

❧

One recurring conversation that every child has with adults contains the big question:"What are you going to be when you grow up?" Our visions of ambition, possibilities, and success come from lots of places. Few of us consider birth order to be a help or a hindrance, but wouldn't it have been dandy to hear how some other little sisters had made it big? What kind of inspiration might they have served? How high can we little sisters hang our stars?

It's no surprise that lots of women who are little sisters have made an impact on culture. These women are active in the media, politics, the arts, and sports. Some of them have set records. Some have pursued their talents and interests—often with the help and support of family—into highly successful careers. Some have advocated unpopular views on controversial issues. Our childhoods, as we shall see later, often prepare us for exercising extraordinary holding power. Here is a sampling of some women who are little sisters:

Gracie Allen—comedian, actor

Maya Angelou—poet and novelist (Named by her brother, incidentally, who called her "mya sister.")

Tallulah Bankhead—actor

Mariah Carey—popular singer

Rachel Carson—writer, conservationist

Edna Ferber—author

Judy Garland—singer, actor

Dorothy Gish—actor

Whoopi Goldberg—comedian and actor

Goldie Hawn—comedian and actor

Aung San Suu Kyi—Burmese dissident who won the 1991 Nobel Peace Prize

Kim Novak—actor

Jane Pauley—television news program host

Being Little Makes a Difference

Most little sisters—from teenagers to women in their seventies—had no doubt that, regardless of how they'd developed, being last made some kind of difference, and often continues to make a difference, in who they are and how they behave.

❧

So what does our birth placement do for us? To discover and refine our little sister identity, we can look at some elements of personal histories and examine some of the research on birth order. The findings are both predictable and surprising.

Some little sisters are conventional. Others rebel in every possible way. Some of us are like our siblings. For those of us who are different from our siblings, we are often *so* dissimilar in such a *variety* of ways as to make our parents rethink the cabbage patch theory of childbirth. (Those who didn't grow up believing that a stork brought babies often thought infants were harvested from the cabbage patch.)

Since we came to our families last, we had to spend a long time trying to puzzle out who was in charge, what everything meant, and, of course, how to get attention and food. No small task when you're little—not just little, but *last*. Regardless of the size of our families, everyone else was there before we were and therefore had at least one less person to cope with as they made their way in life.

In addition to developing survival tools for life management later than everyone else, another feature of our being last was that every single one of the people in our family had immense power—long before we were able understand the situation at all—to toy with us, to try to make us do and learn things they wanted us to do and learn. And they used it, too, didn't they? One little sister reports her brother, four years older, set up the "Jackson Car Club" when she was six. Purpose? To cut out magazine pictures of cars. Membership? Him and her. Chair? Him, of course! Many times, though, our older siblings took pride in teaching us useful skills. This same woman reports that her big brother helped her sound out words when she was dying to learn how to read.

But remember that there was plenty of mischief, too. Sometimes, to them, we were like a new pet, trailing wherever they led. But, to us, they were like multiple bosses! Small wonder we've had to work hard to find our own way.

And then there are the late-arriving little sisters who were coddled and pacified at every turn. Arriving so late, such little sisters were looked upon as *everybody's* baby and received more attention than most babies receive in two-parent families! Great. In addition to the multiple parents, another possibility that often improved the lives of late babies was a change in the family's economic situation. Because the parents were older and more established in their work, sometimes resources were much more plentiful by the time the lastborns came along. Caboose babies, therefore, often experienced virtually no competition for space, love, or nutrition. Good for us; *some* of us. But many little sisters with closer siblings believe that finding a place in the family took fortitude, muscle, and mental gymnastics—and we like to think that our labors contributed to both our character and our strength.

It must be said that some people think that birth order plays a large role in who we are, while others totally dismiss the notion saying that it means nothing at all. Most of the little sisters who spoke to me—from teenagers to women in their seventies—had no doubt that, regardless of how they'd developed, being last made some kind of difference, and often continues to make a difference, in who they are and how they behave.

A Few Moments with Al

*Adler is hailed as the pioneer thinker on birth order as it
relates to the shaping of the personality.*

❧

For centuries, birth order has been used as a guide for
making decisions about whom children would marry or
which vocations sons would follow—military or religious service, for instance, or who would accede to the
throne. In some countries, the law still provides that firstborn sons enjoy special inheritance rights.

People didn't begin paying attention to birth order
as a developmental influence until the psychoanalyst
Alfred Adler wrote about it in 1918. Adler is hailed as the
pioneer thinker on birth order as it relates to the shaping
of the personality. Adler grew up in Switzerland and,
once he was established, became a colleague of Sigmund
Freud. After about a decade, Adler and Freud developed
disagreements on some issues, including the power of the
subconscious. Unlike Freud, Adler viewed humans as social
beings and believed that people operated on a conscious
level rather than being driven primarily by subconscious
urges. Adler and Freud parted ways, and each pursued
theories that continue to be valued and studied.

Regarding the impact of birth order on human development, Adler believed that each time a new child is brought into the home, the environment shifts to accommodate that child. He said, "It is a common fallacy to imagine that children of the same family are formed in the same environment....The psychological situation of each child is individual and differs from that of others. . . ."[1] Adler didn't concern himself with the specific place number in large families, but he did distinguish among firstborns, middleborns, and lastborns.

It is a benefit to us little sisters to consider what Adler had to say about our elder siblings. In observing the behavior and development of firstborns, Adler was struck by the dramatic displacement experienced by them when a newcomer arrived. He referred to the loss of only-child status as "dethronement." Pondering that thought, we little sisters (in families of two children) "dethroned" our big brother or big sister when we came along. Without even trying. It's easy to imagine that the firstborn's feelings of displacement may have had some influence on some of the behavior we later experienced at their hands. Need I say more?

Because of their dethronement, Adler believed, firstborns dwell on the past. Our arrival causes them to experience a loss that they compensate for by focusing on power and authority. Their desire to be in charge becomes a primary issue for them.

Adler described lastborns as going through some of the opposite experiences as the firstborn ones. We lastborns have no new followers nipping at our heels or gaining the attention of parents. Instead, we have many pacesetters to try to keep up with. To have no followers may certainly have some benefits, but to have many pacesetters—parents *plus* siblings—can be quite a challenge and, sometimes, quite a benefit.

(Apropos of probably nothing, but nevertheless fascinating, is the fact that Adler's parents were each the youngest of thirteen (!) children.)

After Adler, theories began to surface about what birth order meant for personalities and development. As you may know, most of the publicized research done on birth order has focused on first children. The firstborns, poor kids, have to put up with more pressure, but they are more likely to get the blue ribbons, the big grants, the Nobels. Part of the reason for their successes is that they tend to be conventional and more driven to achieve. Because of the ways first children are treated and the expectations held for them, they are more likely to behave in acceptable ways with acceptable goals. They are out there getting the money to do the research and having lunch with the publishers or the producers or the politicians.

You can imagine, too, that many books, articles, and monographs have been devoted to exploring the reasons for the grand and successful lives of our firstborn sibs. But how many books have been devoted exclusively to pondering the circumstances and lives of little sisters? One. And you hold it in your hands. It's a beginning.

Alfred Adler's observations of lastborns led him to describe our virtues as well as our imperfections. Adler saw lastborn children as being less self-confident and more likely to resort to whining, cooperation, pleading, and appealing to parents (usually because of our smaller size and reduced amount of power, I should think). We tend to be more altruistic, more empathetic, more peer-oriented, less identified with parents, and less ready to accept their authority. We're also unconventional, adventurous, rebellious, and likely to be risk takers. Do these adjectives—to one extent or another—describe you as a little sister?

The results of a good deal of research support Adler's theories and observations, but who's surprised? As children, we are sometimes rather desperate to get our way, and we resort to a variety of tactics. One could put that into a positive light by saying that we're ever so resourceful.

The fact that many of us flout authority fits quite well with our strengths. Unconventional. Adventurous. Rebellious. Risk takers. Those are the virtues of explorers, heroes from fairy tales, and those fun people at the office.

Patterns into Adulthood

Learning how not to make decisions is a lesson
that too many of us are taught and have to work
to correct in adulthood.

❦

Those varied characteristics that Adler ascribes to us as children are still with us in our adult lives. Who hasn't witnessed a scene with a whining child and felt an immediate recollection of trying to persuade a brother to return a toy or begging a parent to be allowed to go to the late movie. Surely most little sisters can recall an occasional sense of powerlessness. My family will not be allowed to forget my eighth birthday when my brother and my father decided that the movie we would see would be *On the Waterfront*. I don't remember what I wanted, but I know it wasn't that movie, and it took me years to forgive Marlon Brando, not to mention my father and brother, for wrecking my birthday celebration.

Despite years of maturing and despite the many ways that little sisters learn to conquer the dynamics of their childhood, sometimes the patterns we grew up with find a way to stretch right into adulthood.

Hillary, who has three older sisters—ten, eight-and-a-half, and four-and-a-half years older—describes a little sister effect that she continues to live with: "Since I am the youngest, I wasn't involved in making decisions. I was never consulted when we went on trips or anything. To this day, I find it's hard to make decisions. Even simple things, like where to eat, I'd rather have someone else decide. And it's the same with bigger decisions."

Learning how *not* to make decisions is a lesson that too many of us are taught and have to work to correct in adulthood. One thing that helps us to correct ourselves is to recognize that some of our problems are the result of unnecessary reactions.

Lois also saw patterns of childhood behaviors surfacing in adulthood. Her two older sisters took care of her a great deal as she was growing up, sometimes with parental permission and sometimes just because they wanted to. The lessons seem to have taught her a number of roles, which she adopts in her adult life. For instance, she takes on the roll of "big sister" with people in her graduate program, but can also easily act as the "laid-back little sister" when she wants to. Part of the reason for her shifting roles may be due to an attribute that she picked up as a little sister—a desire for justice: "I notice that I have trouble with unfair treatment in classes; one person shouldn't get more of an audience than everyone else."

Laura and her sister both enjoyed music a lot while they were growing up. She and her sister were highly competitive. Laura played in the high school orchestra; her sister played in the band. In adulthood, her sister has continued with her music and plays professionally. Laura, however, pushed music out of her life entirely for a while, then realized that she was depriving herself of something she enjoyed: "I'm not playing instruments now, but I have music around me, and I've come to accept that it's an important thing for me, too."

For many of us who had competitive relationships with our siblings, we might feel some lingering effects in adulthood. We may find that we do or don't attach ourselves to an activity or behavior or belief because of what our siblings did or didn't do. It's an unconscious form of rebellion that many of us are relieved to let go of, once we recognize its roots and its uselessness to us.

Sorting out Our Siblings

The challenge of sorting out who our siblings were and how they operated provided an ongoing lesson through childhood.

❧

In our early years, we try to sort out and identify who we are and who we will become. This complex puzzle is fed by adults, who have a tendency to make conversation with children by asking them what they're going to be when they grow up. While we stew over our futures, we also think about our big brothers and big sisters: Why are they sometimes so sweet or such a bother or so oblivious to us? What causes their behavior? Why are they so weird sometimes?

Rosalind recalls, "When I was about six and my brother was fifteen, we shared a room until my parents built a new room for me—which was huge, by the way, much larger than my brother's. We shared a set of bunk beds, he on top, me on bottom. One night I opened my eyes to see my brother go flying by me—in a horizontal position. He hit the floor and lay there, very still. I thought he was dead, and went screaming into my parents' room: 'Michael's dead! Michael's dead!' Well, it turned out he wasn't dead, he was still asleep!"

We didn't know if we should imitate them (certainly not Michael). Sometimes we tried it and found ourselves in trouble. Or we obeyed the commands of older siblings, which also got us into trouble. So we tried ignoring them, and you know this behavior, too, could lead to trouble. *"Tootie," Mom says, "didn't your big sister tell you to wash up for dinner?"*

The challenge of sorting out who our siblings were and how they operated provided an ongoing lesson through childhood. Sometimes their guidance was invaluable in directing us either toward what we absolutely wanted to imitate or what we definitely wanted to avoid.

When the Big Ones Bugged Us

Or sometimes it seemed that they bugged us simply to keep us in our place and remind us who had the power.

❧

One experience that seemed common for little sisters, and for little brothers, too, was being "tortured" to one extent or another by older brothers and sisters—especially those within a few years of age to us. Sometimes the torment involved prolonged or repetitive physical overpowering. Often it was a form of manipulation that served the interests of the siblings. Other times it was teasing of some sort or other that ranged from a quick and innocuous game of "keep away" to moments of psychological terror. (Shame on those big kids!) It was an expected event that wound through many childhoods like a stream.

Bigger kids found it useful to be mean to little kids for a few fundamental reasons. They wanted something the younger kid had (box of crackers, telephone, information). They wanted us to do something (go to the kitchen for a snack, bring them the *TV Guide*, keep their secrets). Or sometimes it seemed that they bugged us simply to keep us in our place and remind us who had the power. That type of annoyance included the walk-by punch. We couldn't defend ourselves because it was just unexpected enough, and we couldn't swing back because they were too quickly out of range, or because if we succeeded, they'd come back for retribution. Some little sisters, it should be noted, were fearless in this situation and swung back every time, with disregard for the consequences. Yes, some of us were very tough, very early.

I have found that my own memories of being punched and tortured by my brother serve as just another family memory retold around the kitchen table, a situation that I imagine is true for lots of little sisters.

One of the actions I remember clearly was the jab. This little game was brief and seemed to fill time if my brother, Jerry, was a little bored and we were in the same room. He stiffened his hands so they were shaped like large arrowheads, bent himself into a boxer's stance, sent one arrow swiftly into my rib cage, feigned a second jab, and, while I haplessly placed myself in what I hoped was a defensive position and busied my hands with some effort of fierce reprisal, he zapped his first hand, harpoon-like, into my stomach. A hit. Success. This physical triumph occurred a thousand times during our growing-up years if it happened once. I never did learn how to defend myself. Unlike boys, who often practice this form of play as a natural way of passing time, my girlfriends and I didn't engage in boxing or wrestling for fun, so there was no real opportunity for improvement. I was simply available as a target over and over and over.

Diane says her brother, too, always won the "gotcha last" games (those games that involved punching, where one kid tried to be the last one to pop the other). But a small justice was noted by Diane, "My parents believed anything I said." When she wanted to tell on her brother, she could count on parental comfort. (I admit I, too, enjoyed hearing Jerry scolded, "Be nice to your sister.")

The other side of being saved was that parental intervention also meant the game was up. Sometimes such an ending was welcome, but there were times that I regretted the interruption. I spoke to other little sisters who felt bad when parents rescued them from big brothers or sisters. It was as if an opportunity to be brave or courageous had been taken away.

Amy took the "being bugged" experience and turned it on its head by learning from her older brother how to play rough. Then she found herself in trouble over it. "We were visiting the new kids on the block—their dad was a pastor, no less. There were a couple of boys about my age—elementary school. I wasn't about to be bested by any of them. Apparently I thought the best defense was a good offense, so apropos of nothing, I took one of the boys down and sat on him. Fortunately, our moms didn't get too upset, just made me apologize and explain to the boy that I didn't mean it. And we were all friends after that."

The physical batting that kids get involved in becomes—for some of them—almost a form of conversation without words. After some years, when everyone is more verbal, a lot of the hits and pokes give way to teasing and other mental games. This progression shouldn't be construed as being an ultimate solution, since teasing can bug us, too. When we're a little older, though, we may not find ourselves equipped to fight back physically as

Amy was, but our language skills and confidence level may provide us with the stuff we need to quip back to them in kind.

Learning to Get Along

In the Bowling Green study, little sisters with big brothers most often said that they achieved their goals by using, in order, flattery (clever of us), the help of other children or of parents, and prayer.

❧

Thank goodness for adulthood, but childhood is an inescapable phase. We couldn't sleep through it, and who would want to? It was often so interesting. Despite all the fun (for some, the word *fun* could be read sarcastically), a common element for many of us in those years was squabbling with our siblings. For children nearer in age especially, the close quarters we shared, and the necessity of competing for what we wanted often led to disagreements. Details of these common childhood disputes fade from our memories, so I was pleased to run across a study of ninety-five fifth- and sixth-graders in Bowling Green, Kentucky, who described how they got what they wanted.

The children in the study confirmed what we little

sisters have always known—that oldest siblings are bossy (especially the brothers) and manipulative (the sisters). The big brothers said—I'd be inclined to use the word "admitted" or "confessed" here—they got what they wanted from their younger sisters by bossing, chasing, wrestling, playing tricks, spooking, and teasing. Older sisters got what they wanted by taking turns, explaining reasons, using the excuse of gender (e.g., girls do things they're asked to do), and, finally, bossing. Other strategies that didn't rate as highly included tickling, breaking or messing up things, pretending to be sick, and making the littler sister feel guilty.[2] (Ah, such sweet times.)

Older sisters, at least in this study, certainly set an example of using more civilized methods of getting what they wanted. If we imagine the influence of our older siblings on our attitudes and behaviors and look again at the list of coercive methods according to gender, it's not surprising that other studies show that little sisters who have big brothers are more often described as tomboys than little sisters of big sisters.[3] We learned to react in kind, and older brothers made many of us tougher than we would have been if we'd been coping with big sisters.

The other side of the story, of course, is ours. What strategies did we little sisters use to get what *we* wanted? In the Bowling Green study, little sisters with big brothers most often said that they achieved their goals by using, in order, flattery (clever of us), the help of other children or of parents, and prayer. Then came crying, pouting, or sulking. The final tools were scratching or pinching and actually *complaining* to parents.[4] Presumably, seeking the help of parents is less dramatic and disruptive than actually complaining to them.

There seems to be a hierarchy in relationships with older brothers on a scale that measures strength of character and self-control. We can analyze this continuum of behavior as it moves from managing the situation to experiencing helplessness. First, we little sisters began seeking our way by trying to manipulate, then we tried to gain support from others. If these strategies didn't work, we got involved emotionally, from expressions of disappointment and frustration, down to angry actions that may have caused a detrimental backlash. Finally, we abandoned hope and simply turned our case over to higher authorities. I have to say that it doesn't seem too difficult to think of parallel behaviors in adulthood. (We adults like to think we behave in such a different fashion from children, but maybe we shouldn't be so smug.)

Our behavior toward older sisters was somewhat different. The little sisters in the study threatened to tell on their sisters, or they cried, pouted, or sulked. They also scratched or pinched, and, finally, they resorted to seeking help from parents. All of the behaviors except for bringing parents into the fray had the same statistical clout. I suspect that the behaviors of little sisters toward their big sisters reflect, in part, the way the older sisters treat the little sisters.

Most of the tactics used by little sisters in their interactions with older siblings involved the dynamics of the siblings themselves (except for prayer). The exception in the list is a reliance on the intervention of parents. I think if we look back to our own early days we can conjure up moments of dispute. Sometimes we knew parents were in earshot and could offer assistance without our even having to solicit them. The next level was where we called out "MOMMmmy" or "DAAaaad" to raise their attention to our needs. From there, it fell into deliberate complaints about unfair treatment or pain suffered.

From the parents' viewpoint, it seems common to advise little sisters who are experiencing torture from an older sibling that they should simply ignore them and— zing!—the big sibling will stop being a jerk. On the face of it, the advice is sound. But those adults dishing out the advice do not have someone double their weight sitting on their stomachs or snatching their beloved things and racing off on much longer legs into distant areas of the neighborhood.

I suspect parents think they're doing a favor when they don't intervene. Perhaps these torturous experiences are supposed to help us build character, perhaps they're supposed to teach us to be as tough as our siblings. Sometimes it works that way. It did for Amy, who learned it so well that she got in trouble picking on neighborhood boys. Unfortunately, many of us don't have the resources to learn the lesson in quite that way. Rather, we desperately use any defense at hand—thus the biting and scratching—which often leads to our being further hurt or harassed. Does anyone remember a parent saying to the big sibling, "Now remember you know much more about these power games; help your sister learn your tactics so you can play fairly." I don't think so.

In the world of sibling relationships, one of the meanest (yet awfully clever) tricks we can suffer is when siblings threaten to do something. We don't know if they actually will, but we're not sure we can trust that they won't. Ursula lived with such a burden. "When they wanted things from me," she said, referring to her two older sisters, "they threatened to cut my long hair off." Ursula, in her youthful naïveté, concocted what she thought was a perfect solution. "At night I braided it and put it under my pillow, thinking it would be safer. But I soon realized the tactic wouldn't work. In fact, the braid would make it that much easier for them to do one snip and get it all."

As we experienced these dynamics of getting along— or not getting along—with our siblings and explored how we could and could not get what we wanted, we learned a lot about problem solving, about who tolerates what, and about ways to alter our tactics. The benefits just keep coming at us.

Don't Give Up

Despite the complicated relationships we have with our siblings, it seems that in adulthood a lot of us have warm and loving bonds with our big sisters and big brothers; they can be our most reliable and steady friends.

❧

It is important—crucial, really—to remember that little sisters have all sorts of experiences. Some little sisters feel totally adored by their siblings, and their childhood remains a foundation from which they flourish. Lots of these sisters feel so close to older siblings in childhood that one of their largest sufferings occurs when older siblings move away.

"When I was nine, my brother went off to college, far away in another state," Molly says. "I was devastated. I didn't have a lot of friends as a child and I missed him terribly. I still saw him in the summer, but he was busy with his friends and girlfriends, and then his marriage and children. Then I went off to school and didn't really see him much. It wasn't until I was in my mid-twenties that we were able to really get together and talk as adults. We realized anew how much we liked each other and enjoyed each other's company. It was a double treat for me, because I love his wife, too—she is the sister that I didn't ever think I would have."

Amy recalls that her brother left for college when she was in seventh grade. "I missed him dreadfully," she says. "He was my ally against our parents—you know, two of them, two of us. After he was out of the house, I was outnumbered." He wrote occasionally from college. "Boy, was I proud to get those letters! My big brother, writing to me! Not that he ever told me much about what was going on with him—but I sure treasured the letters. When he signed them 'Love, Your Brother,' I could have died for joy."

After Amy's parents died, she discovered her mother's teenage diary. There Amy found out her mother also was devastated when *her* older brother left home. "Her older brother left the house at twenty-one to get married, and for a few weeks there's all this pain in her diary, almost like the light had gone out of her life. I was so surprised to find I had this in common with her—this feeling bereft when your older brother leaves home. I think younger sisters are in love with their older brothers in a certain way, so when the older ones leave the house, it leaves an enormous hole in a little sister's heart."

Not all of us felt such closeness with our siblings, but we've experienced glimmers of deep caring that mean a great deal to us. Delores recalled a difficult time in her life, when her brother unexpectedly offered her support. "My father became terminally ill when I was eighteen years old, which I've since learned is a very difficult time to lose a parent. I still remember walking down the hallway of the hospital, just after seeing my dad. I was extremely upset. My big brother put his arm around me in a way that he never had before. I found that enormously comforting."

(In addition to Delores's comment that losing a parent in the late teen years is difficult, Walter Toman, a leader in birth order research, says that little sisters of older brothers are more disturbed by the loss of loved ones than little sisters of older sisters or children in other birth order placement. This may be due to these lastborn daughters being strongly connected to men, even though the relationships with them can cause stress as well as comfort and security.[5] Delores's extreme pain may have been because she was the younger sister of an older brother.)

A less traumatic example of unexpected closeness is provided by Diane, who experienced a connection with her brother during very different conditions: Diane is the younger sister of a brother who is four-and-a-half years older. Their childhood tangles were typical. She wanted to be an accepted part of his circle of friends and trailed after them when they played, staying just out of their sight on a courtyard staircase but near enough to feel she was part of what was going on. As they grew older, Diane pestered her brother to get her a date with his friends. All for naught. He finally graduated from high school and went off to college. That shift in his life gave him the confidence to reconsider how he related to his little sister. When he came home for vacation, he performed what ought to be called "the miracle of big brothers"—*he invited Diane to go out with him and his friends for a pizza*. This invitation seems like one of the easiest and most nondescript things in the world, but Diane's comment about the event will resonate with some of the little sisters reading this book:"It was the nicest thing he ever did for me."

The *nicest* thing. And believe me there wasn't a hint of sarcasm in her voice when she told me this story. I wanted to scream, "DIANE!—the nicest thing?" But how could I chastise her? My own eyes were growing wet. I was moved.

Her brother's step into maturity was a sign of things to come. When Diane's parents became ill, her brother requested that his corporation transfer him, which they did. He uprooted and moved his family so that he could assist his parents as their health failed. "He was able to be right there," Diane says. "I have nothing but good things to say about him," she adds. She looks back on their child-hood disputes with a wisdom that reflects the changes that she and her brother have gone through. "Back then, he just wanted me to leave him alone."

Despite the complicated relationships we have with our siblings, it seems that in adulthood a lot of us have warm and loving bonds with our big sisters and big broth-ers; they can be our most reliable and steady friends. (Maybe that's why, when I met a young man recently and asked him if he had a little sister, he said, "No, I wish I did.")

We can't deny, though, that there are many oddities about sibling relationships. There we were, growing up in similar surroundings that may have altered from year to year by economic or social conditions. We share genes, which may or may not give us predilections for similar skills or talents, or mannerisms, or likes and dislikes. Our personal preferences are largely prescribed by the national and media-dominated cultures and also by the small cultures of family and of friends. Our expectations of each other and of ourselves are embedded in some ancient code while at the same time seeming to be rewritten by the demands of the moment. Yet, it is often the case that we siblings emerge into vastly different kinds of lives, spreading ourselves around the globe and across all manner of careers and societies. With regard to the old saying about being able to choose your friends but not your relatives, we should perhaps be pleased and somewhat amazed that so many of us find both friendship and love in the relationships we have with our older brothers and sisters.

For those little sisters who are still hoping for better times, the message is: Don't give up. For those who gave up long ago, the message would have been (and continues to be): Do what's best for you.

What About Our Parents?

*Can we know all of the factors that fed into our parents'
decisions about child rearing? Probably not.*

❧

When we consider the development of ourselves in light
of being little sisters, we can't help but think about life
with our siblings and their influences on us. However,
siblings supply only part of the picture. Two other key
players are our parents. Moms and dads get a great deal
of credit and/or blame for what occurs in our early lives
and whatever the resulting effects that we carry with us
from then on. This book is not designed to focus on
theories of parental influence; however, there are some
findings and ideas that relate parents' behavior to the ways
that siblings in their respective families interacted. Some
of these ideas may be useful to us in understanding more
about the way our particular upbringing was or was not
like the upbringing of other little sisters.

Of course, in addition to looking at studies done on
other people, we have to consider life in our own family.
How did we feel about the treatment our parents gave
each of us? Did we feel that our parents were indulgent,
flexible, overprotective? Did we understand why our

parents behaved as they did? Can we know all of the factors that fed into our parents' decisions about child rearing? Probably not. But we can look at some of the research and consider how it does or does not fit our own situations. Parents, it turns out, indulged us youngest kids less during feeding, according to a study done by R. R. Sears (another prominent name in birth order research) and his colleagues.[6] We have to admit this finding is not a big surprise. There was, after all, lots more going on in the house when we arrived. I can imagine a few ramifications from this deprivation. On the face of it, it means fewer "ooooos" and "aaaaahs," fewer affirming smiles, and more "let's get this over with." Hmmm. What effects did this lack of positive attention have on us? At the time, we may have felt a little rushed or noticed that we were looking at Mom more than she was looking at us. But we didn't realize that feeding could have been any different; however, there were people in the house who indeed realized that feeding time could be different. Yes, those big sisters and big brothers who had been slathered with gooey praise for every little morsel that miraculously slipped between their teensy lips. If those firstborns often have an elevated opinion of themselves, it's no wonder: Even their very act of eating was met with awe and amazement.

I actually find the idea of this much attention to matters of such routine business a bit frightening. It makes me think of parents as Hovercrafts™. There may be more advantages than we'd imagined in avoiding that bright, sharp spotlight at feeding time and other quiet moments of the day. Let's pause for a moment of gratitude to our elder siblings for breaking our parents in. (This very benefit was noted by several adult little sisters.)

Sometimes the bright light on our siblings caused us major problems. The story of Jenny captures the epitome of having to pay for the sins of the earlier born. Jenny was a little sister who had severe limits put on her behavior because of the activities of her older siblings. She had sisters ten and seven years older and a brother two years older whose combined shenanigans resulted in several restrictions for Jenny. One sister had to marry early because of an unplanned pregnancy, so a few years later when boys came to visit Jenny, her mother sat in the room or on the porch with the young couple. If Jenny went out, the event was a double date, which included her older brother. Also, her sisters had been such wild drivers—they drag raced on country roads and had an accident that wrecked the car—that Jenny wasn't allowed to get her driver's license until she was eighteen. On top of all of these constraints, Jenny had to wear her sisters' prom dresses. All in all, Jenny regretted not being allowed to have the opportunity to make her own decisions, even though she realizes that her mother was doing her best to protect her.

Nevertheless, this subtle example of privilege/neglect reveals how entwined all family matters are and, unbeknownst to us, how detailed the environment was that played such a role in shaping our identities.

The First Baby Syndrome

Many younger sisters find that their way into the world has been paved by the older brother or sister who was a handful to those green, young parents.

❦

In the midst of considering birth order research of all types, we can't ignore something extremely basic. Researcher after researcher describe a phenomenon that is so well-known to them that they don't even footnote it. What they say is this: The first child has the highest chance of being accepted by parents.[7] Ouch! But, yes, if we've looked closely we may have seen it. We weren't on site to observe our parents as wild and crazy *adults* being transformed into slobbering, doting *parents* when "Numero

Uno" came along, but we've witnessed the "rebirth" again and again. Our elder sibs may have committed bad thing after bad thing and returned time and again to the fold, in prodigal-son style, to the circle of unconditional love, regardless of the shenanigans they've indulged in. The lucky dogs. Such joy surrounded their return that they don't even get a stern look or a mild scolding.

One little sister who understands this behavior perfectly is Laura, although she sees it with a grandparent instead of her parents. "My sister called grandma a year and a half ago on Christmas. Grandma hasn't heard from her since, but I still hear about that call. I send all these letters to Grandma and pay attention to her, and what I hear about is that my sister called her a year and a half ago." We know we're appreciated, but it is impossible to get a sense of "winning" in a situation like this one. You'd think that once in a while we'd abandon family allegiances and behave like those sibling ingrates, but we don't. We can be dreadfully loyal, even when it hurts to do so.

We have to remember, too, that sometimes the first-born was such a hellion that our parents were relieved when we came along. Many younger sisters find that their way into the world has been paved by the older brother or sister who was a handful to those green, young parents. Mimi says about her firstborn, older brother,

"Once, when he was a toddler, he found my mother's bright red lipstick, smeared it all over himself, head to toe, including the bottoms of his feet, and proceeded to walk all around the house." Her mom and dad regarded the girls who followed as "easier babies." Even as adults, Mimi feels that she and her sister have received more acceptance from their parents than her older brother did.

As we hope to be loved enough—if not the most— by our parents, we little sisters can't help but think about the fact that our siblings have been around longer. They've had more years to woo the folks and to bond with them in strong and secure relationships. Most of us work hard to catch up with the ones who arrived first. And for some of us, our small thoughtful deeds—like not making unnecessary messes—may be enough to earn us favor.

Some Early Attributes

I do have to admit that oversensitivity is a useful umbrella for many of our attributes.

❧

In contrast to the oldest sibling being automatically accepted by virtue of being born first, another study that looked at the behaviors of young children shows little sisters in a fairly good light. The study was done in Berkeley, California, for over a dozen years.[8] Researchers interviewed mothers about their children's behaviors and categorized actions into both specific events, such as nail biting and shyness, and into generalized terms, such as mood swings and negativism. See what you think about the daunting list of what our siblings were up to, compared with us virtual cherubs.

The firstborn sons reportedly exhibited the following:
* disturbing dreams
* mood swings
* oversensitivity
* physical timidity
* specific fears
* restless sleep
* attention-demanding actions

Younger brothers reportedly had the following:
* temper tantrums
* overactivity
* jealousy
* lying
* food finickiness
* speech problems
* negativism

* destructiveness
* bed wetting
* insufficient appetite

Oldest sisters reportedly had these features:
* attention-demanding actions
* overactivity
* tics and mannerisms
* shyness
* restless sleep
* somberness
* temper tantrums
* nail biting
* lying
* excessive reserve
* physical timidity
* mood swings
* negativism

By contrast, the list of reported descriptors about little sisters is surprisingly small:
* oversensitivity
* thumb sucking

Only oversensitivity and thumb sucking? So few sins? Were we so perfect? Or were our mothers too exhausted by our siblings' wide-ranging misbehaviors to be coherent when it was time to consider us? I do have to admit that oversensitivity is a useful umbrella for many of our attributes. But let's remember this is research. Statistics—in their superior and sweeping way—can, in fact, be meaningful for hundreds of people but be totally irrelevant to an individual. The oldest brother described here sure wasn't *my* older brother. And the me that's described is a me I would have been happy to be. Where's the shyness? Where's the food finickiness and the suffering it caused me?

The author of the study adds that for little sisters of big sisters, life was undoubtedly easier because mothers would have realized with their first daughter that some of the high expectations were silly and not to be fulfilled.[9] Some of the women I spoke with experienced this effect.

Alfred Adler's theories, as mentioned earlier, of what we lastborns were like further develops this small list of our early behaviors. If you remember, he described us as being less self-confident and more likely to resort to whining, cooperation, pleading, and appealing to parents and found littlest sisters and brothers to be more altruistic, more empathetic and peer-oriented, less identified with parents and less ready to accept their authority. This translated into being unconventional, adventurous, risk-taking, and rebellious. Many of these attributes are wonderful building blocks for rich lives. Our tendency to be generous, combined with a sense of adventure and even rebelliousness, may lead us into fascinating situations that are both personally satisfying and helpful to others. Despite some handicaps that we've had to put up with, little sisters have more to be thankful for than to complain about. However, I happen to think a little well-placed whining and pleading expresses passion, concern, and true desire. Very useful in its place.

How We Fit into the World

Apparently due to our years of contending with our siblings and with their friends, we little sisters are skilled on the sociability scale.

Can these stories and bits of research and ideas begin to help us sort out how being a little sister contributes to our identity? Can we understand ourselves better as adults? Some of us regretfully drag out our little-sister status as blame for the way our lives have gone, and others cheerfully put it on display as a source for things that have been perfect. Although we don't usually obsess about our status as little sisters, the idea comes up from time to time, often with our best friends (particularly those who are themselves little sisters) who listen to our tales over and over and help us as we try to figure ourselves out.

Birth order researcher Lucille Forer compiled numerous findings about little sisters and drew some conclusions for us. Here is her list of criteria for us to consider when we think about how we fit into the world:

✳ **Self-Esteem** How approving are you of yourself?

A high sense of self-esteem comes most naturally to only children; the firstborn (whom we dethroned) have the greatest need for approval. Many of us last children find that the pressure is not nearly as strong as it was for earlier brothers and sisters, and we can thrive. Little sisters of brothers, though, have a more difficult time than little sisters of sisters. Forer says that one of the important issues for little sisters who only have big brothers is that they're not pleased with the feminine part of themselves; they don't even particularly like women. Coming to terms with this aspect of oneself could be a powerful way to raise one's self-esteem.[10]

✳ **Need for Approval** Are you the best judge of the adequacy of what you do, or do you need others to approve?

The need for approval from others, especially authority figures such as parents and employers, is not nearly as important to us as it is to firstborns. But that's not to deny that recognition and praise are important.[11] Considering our tendency toward a rebellious nature, we have to think about this need in terms of specific activities. In some situations, we may feel totally confident to judge our accomplishments, and in others, we may be reliant on the words of others.

✱ **Self-Sufficiency** Are you dependent upon other people for support, comfort, and reassurance?

While this quality overlaps with the first two aspects, it also raises the question of how much support we need. Generally, females who were not the firstborn in their families seem to cope with difficult situations better. If we're alone during a crisis, we are less likely to feel panicked.[12]

✱ **Sociability** Do you *like* being with other people?

Apparently due to our years of contending with our siblings and with their friends, we little sisters are skilled on the sociability scale. Most of us were quite comfortable talking with adults when we were young, and as adults ourselves we're also comfortable discussing personal matters. However, our comfort in being with strangers doesn't carry over to a desire to be part of a club. In particular, little sisters with one older brother are less likely to be joiners, although little sisters of sisters or larger family groups are more apt to join social groups.[13]

�֍ Conformity   Do you feel comfortable when your ideas and behavior differ from others?

If you're the youngest, you probably enjoy holding minority opinions. All indicators show that firstborns are most likely to align themselves with traditional beliefs and goals and to succumb to peer pressure. Of course, the extent of our nonconformity is connected to lots of other factors, such as our peer influences, our ambitions, our political and religious affiliations, our community activities, and so on. Conformity—or the lack of it— also hooks into personal tastes for food, clothing, and leisure activities.

�֍ Morality   How strictly do you adhere to the moral and ethical standards of society?[14]

Don't read this description as if it were asking about major transgressions, such as theft or murder. Think about the finer points, like keeping secrets. We're less interested in keeping them, probably because when we were little, we figured out that they can be a useful tool for bargaining. The trend of telling all continues into later life. We are also more inclined to get into trouble at school and to be called to the carpet in college.[15]

Isn't it grand to be so complicated and filled with seeming contradictions? By exploring our lives and motives and by learning from the experiences of other little sisters, I believe we can eventually make sense of all of it.

Pondering these issues is a process that invites us to travel back along several paths of our personal history. Perhaps we recall beliefs that we held as children or adolescents or remember events that had long been lost to the years between then and now.

Thinking about that early stage of life is entertaining for me. Sometimes it's as if I'm watching a movie, but the little kid looking at her long shadow as she sways back and forth on the swing is me. Sometimes, this position of being last in the family makes me wonder if we little sisters find that our inner child is closer than everyone else's. While the rest of the world worries about trying to get in touch with their inner child, we often wonder what the fuss is about. We see ours every morning—all we have to do is look in the mirror. Many of us—despite our adult maturity—hold tight our memories of ourselves as children, which can be a great benefit as we try to understand those around us. No wonder we're more empathetic with our own children. No wonder we're a lot of fun. In some ways, perhaps we still *are* the children we were.

And sometimes we're still the children who won't put away their clothes, sew on a much needed button, or wash the car. When I do something that belongs to the category of "immature neglect," I have a strong sense that my inner little sister is acting out about something. Take putting away clothes, for instance. When I was young and clothes piled up on my chair, my mom grew irritated. Her cure was either to scold me about it until I did something or clean it up herself when I was in school. So now when I mess up my room, am I being lazy? Am I being childish? Is this chaos that I bring upon myself something worth examining? (Am I simply a slob?) It's nothing I choose to stew over. I've learned that the cycle shifts, and tomorrow or the next day or the day after that, I'll feel more like an adult. I'll empty the chair of its clothes and put everything neatly away. Perhaps someday I'll be a grown-up around the clock, but I rather doubt it. There are lots of activities and preferences I share with children that I'd hate to abandon—like staying outside when it rains or eating potato chips on my ice cream.

Part of the reason to stay in touch with one's early years is to appreciate the connections between then and now. Many of us have what amount to solid bridges between our present and our past. The stories of Ellen and Jane show how some early sensitivities and actions in childhood resonate in their personalities as adults.

Ellen is a kind and considerate young woman with a large group of friends. Her adult behaviors are clearly influenced by her childhood actions. Ellen says she and her sister were never very competitive, although her sister "liked to be in charge." Ramona Quimby, the star character of some of Beverly Cleary's novels, played an important part in Ellen's life: "She was a model to me for how to be a little sister. Once, Ramona called her older sister a pizza face, and the sister became very upset. I didn't want to make my sister that upset, so when we fought, I'd be careful never to call her names. I didn't want to hurt her like that."

Jane is another little sister who recognizes that part of her identity was created by childhood relations. She worked hard in her growing-up years to do anything and everything her older brothers didn't do, but she nevertheless spent a lot of time hanging around with them and their friends. Now, she said, she feels comfortable around men. "I like men a lot," she said. "I like the company of men. And I understand men better because of the time I spent with my brothers' friends when I was young."

I think it can be valuable to occasionally consider how we feel about ourselves in terms of topics such as those suggested by Forer. Most days are so absorbed with the particulars of that twenty-four hour period, that it is rare to pause and contemplate things like our need for approval or how we feel about conformity. If a situation arises that puts the issue right in our face, we can stop and think about it in its immediate context and perhaps let it hang around our minds long enough to consider it in a larger picture. One dividend may be in seeing how we've grown or matured in some areas.

A Surprising Tradition

For instance, there are taboos against his sitting too near his sisters and of telling off-color jokes in their presence.

Just to keep a perspective on the issues of little sister-hood, consider briefly how some customs from a distant culture ensure that little sisters are treated with respect.

In the !Kung tradition, a woman's name links her to every other tribal woman who has the same name, and the woman's brother then thinks of all other so-named women as his sisters. His behavior is altered in his dealings with all of his sisters—as defined by name, not by blood relationship. For instance, there are taboos against his sitting too near his sisters and telling off-color jokes in their presence.[16]

What could such taboos do for us in our culture? First of all, think how we might be saved enormous discomfort and embarrassment if our brothers couldn't be too near us. Imagine it! No poking, pinching, skin burns, hitting, hair pulling, or finger flicking, and no family trips where we're stuck in the back seat next to big brother. And the absence of off-color jokes might be pleasant, too. Ah, well. We have to play the hand we were dealt.

The Vantage Point of Adulthood

As adolescents, many of us were inclined to think that when we reached adulthood, we'd have this or that characteristic as if by magic. It was as though we could select ingredients off a shelf, mix them up, and drink down the designer potion. What we come to realize, notwithstanding the occasional epiphany, is that transformation doesn't occur in a single day. Instead, we understand that as we move from house to house and town to town, following jobs and opportunities and companions, the events, feelings, beliefs, fears, and discoveries of each day cling to us and contribute, bit by bit, to who we are and who we are becoming.

Whether the memories of our childhoods as little sisters are sweet or painful—and for most of us they are some of each—the effects of our birth order remain with us long after we've left the family home. No clear and tidy summaries offer a rigid design that presses little sisters into one mold, though researchers have tagged some common traits of little sisters. Most of us would find that several of the labels suit us well. For instance, we are adventurous and rebellious, although some of us struggle with issues of confidence and self-esteem. We are often seen as flexible and relaxed; we're also popular, and some of us are "daddy's favorite." Sometimes we suffer from lack of attention and sometimes we suffer from an excess of the same thing. We grew up in the shadows of our older brothers and sisters, which can endow us with a permanent state of delight or send us racing to escape the family setting as soon as possible. And many of us experienced a full range of interactions with our older siblings who were good, naughty, funny, sweet, and more.

Everything that happens to us mingles with our inherited characteristics as we develop. The multiplicity of little sisters is vast, despite common experiences. Even those of us who feel very similar in our histories and our outlooks recognize that many facets of our personalities differ. With all of the possibilities that exist, how could it be any different? And yet, in the wealth of experiences that little sisters may have, we often find that we share a good portion of them with other little sisters that we meet.

By bringing into our conscious minds the patterns of behavior that we learned in childhood, we may uncover some surprising and useful information. Some of those patterns may continue to serve us well, and others may have worn out their usefulness long ago. As we understand more about our history, we find ways to take steps that may have seemed impossible in our child's mind.

Adulthood, for little sisters, is a time to build borders, set limits, and develop increased self-confidence. The process of delineating ourselves clearly may be a slow one, because, even if we change substantially in our thinking about family matters, the rest of the family may not be following along. When we're with family members or communicating with them, we find ourselves clarifying our new territory one brick at a time. Sometimes it takes years. And so it goes.

Meanwhile, we can take care of ourselves by exercising privileges of adulthood. We can work hard at our jobs, our avocations, or our hobbies—whatever gives us satisfaction. We can enjoy our family members and friends. We can give of ourselves, which comes naturally to a lot of little sisters. We can pursue a spiritual life. We can take care of the pieces of us that we fear were neglected or somehow left behind. Arriving at the party last is not necessarily a bad thing. After all, no matter how old we grow, our siblings will always be older than we are. No matter how many decades we accumulate, we'll always have youth—and its tendencies toward energy, enthusiasm, curiosity, and hope—on our side.

CHAPTER TWO

How Do We Feel About Ourselves?

Anybody ever tell you you're a cute little trick?

– *THE LITTLE SISTER*, RAYMOND CHANDLER –

Elizabeth Taylor is a little sister of the most indomitable sort. From her regal Cleopatra to her performance decades earlier in *National Velvet* as a spunky, young horse lover determined to conquer impossible odds, Taylor's film characters often reflected the same spirit she possessed through difficult times in her personal life. Through her multiple marriages and early public work for AIDS research, she's conveyed an impassioned certainty that reveals a high degree of self-confidence. Regardless of how you may feel about Ms. Taylor, her grace and courage during sorrowful times of illness, bereavement, and divorce, under extraordinary public scrutiny, call for admiration. Ms. Taylor's strength seeps from her pores, and we should keep her in mind when we need to call upon the "little sister goddesses" for a boost.

Self-Esteem, Self-Esteem, Where Did You Go?

Some of the research on characteristics of the lastborn would indicate that low self-esteem, at least for parts of our lives, is not too surprising.

❧

While most of us little sisters enjoy mature and healthy self-esteem in adulthood (once we've figured out a few things), a good many of us wandered aimlessly around in our youth, feeling good about ourselves one day and awful the next. Part of it is the angst that accompanies adolescence, but part of it has to do with what the world expects of us. At this stage our world is largely our family, our friends, and our teachers. But it is in the family where we first learn how to act and react. It is in the family where we feel cherished by siblings one moment and taunted by them the next, where we may experience lavish attention at some points and simple neglect at others.

Some of the research on characteristics of the lastborn would indicate that low self-esteem, at least for parts of our lives, is not too surprising. One obvious reason for the slumping esteem is that, at least for a while, we're the least knowledgeable one in the house. "Some youngest children, especially women, may lack self-confidence, as they were overly protected and felt inferior when competing with the older children," says one researcher.[1] This single finding sums up a state of affairs that is familiar to many little sisters.

Recently I was speaking with a grown-up little sister who witnessed a classic little sister moment a few days earlier. It resonated strongly with her, as it does with me.

Marcia was having dinner with a friend of hers who is the father of two children—a teenage boy, Ted, and a six-year-old daughter, Sophie. The topic of the Beatles came up during dinner. Sophie is a fan. Ted, taking on the "older and wiser" role, commented, "Oh, they're so, you know, so British." Sophie was indignant. Her response: "They are not British. They're English." The son and father hooted with laughter, while Marcia offered comfort to Sophie. "I was the only one who understood what had happened," she said later. "I remember how, as the youngest, I was made the butt of every joke. It's really hard to be in that position."

Yes, how familiar that feeling is of having the rug pulled out from under us when we thought we had made sense of the world and done away with confusion. What fills me with consternation occasionally is that the familiar feeling has still not evaporated. Will I ever know enough not to feel left out? Will I ever be absolutely sure that I'll never experience another rug-pulling event? For some of us, feeling ignorant when we were young inspired a lifelong search for knowledge and understanding. Amy, younger of two in her family—but, even more important, youngest of all her first cousins—remembers being laughed at during extended family get-togethers. "My next cousin, a boy, was only a few months older than me, but he positioned himself with the older kids," she says. "I remember all of them making fun of me when I mispronounced a word or something like that."

How did Amy cope? She embarked on a quest to understand as much about the world as she could—and last year she completed her Ph.D. "I didn't go into graduate school to get back at my older brother or my cousins," she assures me. "I didn't even think about them. But I do remember, when I was really little, wanting to get over this feeling that everyone around me understood more about the world than I did." Her education has made all the difference.

By contrast, Christine had a great start as a little sister. Her brother is seven years older than she is, and Christine felt both loved and respected by him. He even consulted her about personal decisions. "Once he asked me about two women he was seeing. He was about twenty-five, and he was evidently trying to decide who to spend his life with. I let him describe both women, and what he liked about each of them. As I could see that he was leaning toward the woman whom I adored, I enthusiastically supported her as my favorite, too. He ended up marrying her. I'm sure that I didn't make up his mind for him on the issue, but it made me feel proud that he thought my opinion was important." Chritine says that experiences such as this one contributed to the strong sense of self-esteem she enjoys as an adult.

Little sisters' self-esteem is composed of many elements and an assortment of moments from life. Some little sisters seem to be born into a state of self-assurance, and the condition stays with them into adulthood. Other little sisters work toward a stronger self-esteem bit by bit, two steps forward and one step back. As we strive to feel confident about ourselves and about our actions, we are sometimes hindered by our older siblings and sometimes helped by them. So it goes.

Catching Up

We watched our older siblings endlessly, figuring out how they did this thing called life.

Rare is the little sister who didn't feel she had to work hard to keep up with older siblings. The big brother or big sister who had to win throughout the day tended to keep us on our toes. This force in the house taught us important survival tactics that often became part of our personality as we learned how to carve out our own niche in life, to make our own way apart from others. But unlike oldest children, who have to do this all by themselves, we did it in response to older sisters and brothers. We watched our older siblings endlessly, figuring out how they did this thing called life. Sometimes we tried it their way; then we switched tactics to try something very different from whatever they did. As we grew, we fine-tuned the balancing act that defined our space in the family. We decided when to give in and when to be demanding, we sought and nurtured alliances that flourished or failed, and we developed the behaviors that helped us get the attention we needed. The result of this myriad of actions and characteristics contributed to our own style and personality. Some facets of our behavior (Were you stubborn? Were you shy?) stayed with us into adulthood, but others shrank away when they no longer served us. Finding the balance that serves us in adulthood is not generally a one-time event. Circumstances change, and we have to locate that balance again. And sometimes again.

Katherine remembers building her confidence by observing her sister, Barb, who was a year-and-a-half older. "I remember when Barb got her driver's license and started going out on dates. She'd come home late, and I'd watch her weasel out of getting punished. I learned how to get around Mom and Dad by watching her." Katherine also remembers "getting tips" on various teachers at school, "It helped to have an older sister. I could learn from what worked for her. And I got confidence that I could do it, too."

I learned a little bit about catching up by agreeing to be my brother's chess opponent. Jerry was the only person I ever played with, and I lost to him, so I didn't feel that I had much of an opportunity to improve. I was ten or eleven during this phase, and his playing method was stressful to me; he would consider every move by trying to see how each of us would move two, three, and four turns later. All of this thinking took what seemed like a long time, and I got bored waiting for my turn. I also hated the thought that he knew what I would do for the next several moves. But of course I played with him because I was flattered that he asked, and it was something to do. And I also started spending my wait time trying to understand strategies. The day finally came when I beat him. It happened only once. But, oh that glorious word: "Checkmate." He was dumbfounded, and I left him staring at the board, no doubt playing the game backwards to see where he'd gone wrong and where I'd done something that he hadn't predicted. For me, figuring out strategies and patterns has paid off in play, such as with board games like backgammon, and in life, where I relish figuring out the most efficient routes during high traffic times.

Joyce admits to being an extremely competitive adult—especially around men. She developed her desire to catch up during her childhood when she had two active and successful brothers. She recalls a story from her early adulthood. "I was on a weekend camping trip with my best friend. She had arranged to meet some friends of hers—a married couple—for the day. They brought their bicycles, and we spent the day riding in a state park. Around noon we came upon a small creek. The creek was shallow, but the banks on either side were steep. As we approached the creek my two female companions got off their bikes to do the sensible thing—walk them through the creek. The man, however, just set his jaw and roared on through the creek safely to the other side. I knew he was lucky, that the smart thing to do was to get off my bike and walk through the creek. But instead, all I could think about was doing exactly what he did, so that he couldn't best me. I raced toward the creek, slipped and fell, and almost broke my leg. I still have a picture of my girlfriend and me nursing my wounds." Sometimes our efforts to catch up knock us down. But Joyce got back up. She now competes successfully in the business world, and we might assume that there are times when she decides to "walk her bike across the creek" if it makes good business sense to do so.

Whether the lessons come from our siblings, the world at large, or ourselves, it seems that as we do what we can to catch up with our siblings, we inevitably stumble once in a while. Our desire to do whatever it takes to get ourselves onto their playing field is an attribute that we can make great use of. Being doggedly determined may get us into trouble occasionally, but we all know that if we don't get up to try again, we stay down, and that's the end of it.

Some Childhood Moments

That ego inside of us, which plays such a big role in how we behave, thrives on attention. Proper attention.

❧

In recalling some early events that influenced the growth of your self-esteem, a particular scene may stand out in your mind. Remember sitting at the dinner table while the conversation among your parents and siblings blurred over your head? Perhaps the talk was filled with news about a basketball game or an upcoming recital, or maybe it was her homework or his piano teacher or their need for a new pair of jeans or a dress. Maybe words like "backboard," "soundboard," "blackboard," "sideboard," "billboard," or "school board" came up. You asked what the words meant, but everyone was involved in the conversation, and your question went unanswered.

You were experiencing a phenomenon common to us youngest children. As early as 1945, researcher J. H. S. Bossard saw that in family table conversation, the talk was aimed at the level of the oldest; the interests of the youngest were not only ignored, but their questions about the meanings of words were often ignored, too.[2]

What happens when we're ignored? You don't have

to be a rocket scientist or a little sister to answer this question. Inasmuch as self-esteem is something we gain through our interactions with others, being ignored or chuckled at or condescended to can make our self-esteem plummet. We translate such treatment into a simple message: "My interests and concerns are not important, so I must not be important either."

That ego inside of us, which plays such a big role in how we behave, thrives on attention. Proper attention. We little sisters, who may have been overwhelmed with attention when we arrived, generally remember later moments when we received scanty amounts, especially if we come from larger families. We have to ask ourselves, *Was it was enough to help us thrive? Or was it respectful enough to compensate for the holes?* The issue of the quantity and quality of attention that children need will continue to be debated because, in part, it seems that different children need different amounts. What's sufficient for one child barely covers the bottom of the bucket for another. Does attention equal love? No. But attention is surely one expression of love.

Besides, with the right kind of attention from others, we can do lots of things ourselves to build a positive sense of self. Doing something well is the most common way to build confidence. Mimi remembers, "I took guitar and voice lessons as a teenager—partly because I was interested in them, partly so I could do my own thing apart from my sibs. My brother was a talented artist and my sister was a good student and athlete, and I wanted to be a musician." Mimi studied music for several years and still uses her talent as a singer. "Studying music worked," she says, "in that it made me feel I could do something that my older brother and sister couldn't."

Taking lessons to improve in music or athletics or in the arts has always been a way to strengthen self-esteem. Besides lessons, though, we little sisters enjoyed perfecting various skills at home. Remember who was best at jacks or neighborhood ball games like 7-up, kickball, or horse? What about badminton, jump rope, or self-styled diving at the local pool? Then there were board games or arts and crafts projects, such as designing clothes for our paper dolls or putting on plays for the neighborhood. We explored available activities to find something that was fun and that we did well. Everything counted.

The Older Brother Success Story and Remembering the Phoebes

Sometimes the drive of older siblings can be a boost to little sisters.

❧

Unfortunately, even when we're good at something—even very good, even world class—an older sister or brother can still steal the show. Remember Beth Heiden? She was a little sister who appeared to share the same ambitions as her older and only brother, Eric, and if you're old enough to remember the 1980 Olympic Games, her name is probably familiar to you. She and Eric, who were close as children and while growing up, were also the skating darlings of the Winter Games that year, though it was Eric who took a record number of gold medals. In their hometown, Madison, Wisconsin, the siblings are stars, and they showed their appreciation to the town by having a special warming house built for the city's ice skating residents. By contrast, in the highly reputable *Encyclopedia Britannica,* what do we find? An entry for Eric, which he certainly deserves, that stretches to 103 words. The final nine words are "His younger sister, Beth, was also a world-class skater."[3] A measly 9 percent of the copy is devoted to Beth, and not a single detail of her many accomplishments is included. It's true that her showing at the games was disappointing (a single bronze), but she was a world champion skater in 1979, a world champion in bicycle road racing in 1980, an NCAA champion in cross-country skiing, as well as the U.S. Olympic Committee's Sportswoman of the Year in 1980. These are not tiny accomplishments. Chances are that if she hadn't had an older brother who was so celebrated, we'd have heard more about her. Sorry, Beth.

Sometimes the drive of older siblings can be a boost to little sisters. The Redgraves and the Fondas come to mind, though the encouragement and support of their parents no doubt also played a role. Surprisingly, researcher Lucille Forer found that studies up to the mid-1970s indicated that youngest sisters in small families tended to be relaxed and not particularly motivated to achieve professionally. However, the youngest sisters in large families were said to have watched the examples of their older siblings and be more driven to strive.[4] Well, research is statistical and life is anecdotal. Besides famous lastborn women, I've met and have heard of a lot of women who are little sisters who came of age in the mid-1970s who are driven and working hard for their dreams. And I don't want to omit the accomplishments of little sisters from other times.

Remember Phoebe Fairgrave Omlie? Me neither. In fact, I asked ten people about Phoebe Omlie and no one had any idea who I was talking about. I discovered Phoebe in a book of notable women. She was an aviator of Amelia Earhart's generation, but her tale had a happy ending. And she was a quintessential little sister.

Phoebe was fascinated by flying after attending an air show when she was a young girl. After high school, she tried acting school and a secretarial job, but she was restless. She bought four flights at the local air field, which inspired her to use an inheritance of $3,500 to buy an airplane. What gumption—she didn't even know how to fly! Nevertheless, wanting to regain the value of her purchase, she contacted Fox Moving Picture Studio and sold them an assortment of flying stunts for the price of $3,500. She eventually learned to fly and performed the stunts; they were used in the movie, *The Perils of Pauline.*

Meanwhile, Phoebe, at age seventeen, had a plane she couldn't fly. Most instructors at the local air field wouldn't teach her because she was too small and too young. But Vernon Omlie gave her a shot. Two years later, they married and enjoyed a long life together flying planes and promoting aviation. In addition to flying, Phoebe learned a variety of aerial tricks. At eighteen she was the first woman to do a double parachute drop (one chute opens, it's cut loose, and a second one opens). She later became involved in politics and persuaded Franklin Delano Roosevelt's campaign manager to use a plane in the campaign, which initiated air travel for candidates. And on and on. (Her husband, ironically, was killed in a commercial airplane crash.)[5] Phoebe, as unknown as she is, is a wonderful model for little sisters.

There are lots of other Phoebes for us to appreciate—in history books and in our neighborhoods. Depending upon your age, interests, and region of the country, some of the following names may be familiar to you:

Irene Castle—ice skater and animal care promoter

Genevieve Rose Cline—first woman appointed as a
U.S. federal judge

Ruth Suckow—novelist

Helen Traubel—opera and concert singer

Mabel Vernon—suffragist, feminist, and pacifist

Ask around. The stories are everywhere.

What Can We Do with Ambitious Moms?

Some of us have to negotiate the desires and demands of our parents, whose plans for us sometimes differ from our own aspirations.

While we're trying to discover which things we'd like to be good at and what we want to do in our lives, we may find obstacles other than those laid down by our brothers and sisters. Some of us have to negotiate the desires and demands of our parents, whose plans for us sometimes differ from our own aspirations. (Phoebe's parents, by the way, were split in their opinion of Phoebe's ambitions. She said that her dad thought she was crazy, but her mom supported her whole-heartedly.)

Parents are different in a million ways, but I came across one bit of research on the influence of birth order on parenting that is not too surprising. Mothers who are firstborns tend to be more tense, more driven, and more driving (pushing their children) than laterborn moms.[6] These attributes fit right in with the research on firstborns that says they are high strivers and high achievers. It comes as no further surprise that among the ambitions of firstborn mothers are the lives of their children; children are, after all, one of their accomplishments. First-born daughters tend to take the brunt of a mother's ambitious energies, which often leads to a reality check for mom, and she consequently learns to lighten up. So, little sisters with older sisters may be less subject to their mother's drive.

It may be the case, too, that our firstborn mothers were a valuable boon to us in urging us to accomplish our own great things, but, as mentioned earlier, they could also make us feel as though we could never live up to their ideals. The irony is that, as they urged us to try for the top of the class, the president of the club, at least the most attractively groomed, we didn't realize the reason for the fuss. Many little sisters with pressuring moms believed that they—the little sisters—were inadequate, thus all the pressure. Imagine what a relief it is to realize that it wasn't always us; it was them—their birth order must take partial credit for their driving personalities.

If you're a little sister with a firstborn mother who has always held extraordinarily high ambitions for you, take a fantasy moment to pause and imagine your mother's childhood, her teen years, and her young adulthood. What if you, as a child, had been given this new perspective on your mother's personality? Would some of the friction have been eased? Would you have found yourself, on occasion, nodding in understanding rather than tensing up in defensiveness? It's too bad that we little sisters don't generally give a thought to mum's birth order until we're well into adulthood. Perhaps if we had understood this facet of our mothers earlier, growing up would have been a bit easier. The knowledge may have helped us realize that, to some extent, our mothers (and our fathers!) couldn't help who they were. Just as, to some extent, we couldn't help who we were, and can't help who we continue to be. By knowing more about our parents as well as ourselves, our strengths, and our potential, we can work with greater wisdom toward the ambitions we have for ourselves.

What's in a Name—or a Nickname?

To be fair, we have to realize that these nicknames often began harmlessly.

❧

And then there's the issue of nicknames. How many little sisters complain that their older siblings never let them outgrow the baby names? Take Katherine, for instance. She was "Kathy" when she was little, and she's "Kathy" to her family still, even now that she's forty-one and prefers "Katherine." "Everyone else was able to make the change," Katherine laments. "It's only my family that still insists on calling me Kathy. And it's catching, too. The other day I was at a party where everyone knows me as Katherine. Then my older sister walked into the party and started talking to people. By the end of the party, they were all hollering, 'Bye, Kathy!' as I was leaving. They'd picked it up from her!"

Ursula, youngest of three girls, says that her sisters had lots of nicknames for her that fell into the "stupid" category. But her sisters, like Katherine's, also still call her the baby names, like "Ursy" and other designations that highlight the fact that she is the youngest. "I have no way to change their names to make them silly, too," she said.

To be fair, we have to realize that these nicknames often began harmlessly. Sometimes an older sibling couldn't pronounce our names (and sometimes we couldn't pronounce theirs, creating a nickname that did or didn't stick once our language was clearer). Sometimes the creation or alteration of a name happened simply because we were the last and littlest—a name with y at the end of it (or names like "Peanut" or "Mouse") was meant as an endearment by those who gave it.

On the surface, the idea of a nickname seems innocent enough, but lots of little sisters felt annoyed or hurt by them. Many of the nicknames that we were labeled with were insults or were perceived as insults—often about our physical appearance—even though the taunt may have had nothing to do with reality. My own brother resorted to a foreign tongue, lashing out with "Skuk-shefta," a three-syllable dinger that he put a lot of spit and passion into. The word means "crooked mouth" in Norwegian, or so I was told, but it never made much sense to me. (When we're small, we take things literally.) I checked my mouth in the mirror, and it looked like the same mouth on one side as it did on the other. But his tone could still carry enough weight to make me hang my head—whether or not I should have. Many little sisters have had to bear unwanted comments about their hair, their legs, their faces and all its parts, their necks, their feet, their chests, and anything else that seems useful at the moment to a big brother or big sister.

Melinda is the youngest of five with two older brothers and two older sisters. As she and her sisters began to mature, the brothers had plenty of fun insulting them. Melinda's sisters' breasts began to develop adequately, but her own chest remained as flat as a surfboard, about which attribute she was frequently teased. "The favorite taunt of my brothers was to designate us as 'Pimple,' 'Dimple,' and 'Crater.' I was so humiliated, I used to pray to God

I'd get large breasts some day." Her prayers were answered generously, and she has been careful ever since about what she prays for.

Sometimes brothers strike the opposite note (without resorting to nicknames). Marianne remembers, "I always felt really flattered when my brother would give me praise. I remember one day in my early teens, when Michael was following me through a doorway, and as we were walking along, he said, 'So when did you get such great legs?' I was thrilled to have that affirmation at that really sensitive age, and I have felt great about my legs ever since!"

Finally, we have to remember that endearing nicknames can grow out of treasured moments of playing with older sibs. Mimi, for instance, remembers one weekend when the whole family went on a vacation, and the kids shared a hotel room. She was about nine, her older sister, eleven, and their brother, fourteen. "My brother decided to entertain my sister and me, so he made up this long story about the little green men he said were all over the room, wearing little green hats with feathers in them. We spent the whole evening fantasizing together about who they were, what they were doing, what they looked like. My brother made nicknames for us. Mine was 'Perg,' because he said that's the only way to get rid of little green men, by throwing 'pergs' at them. To this day, thirty years later, he calls me 'Perg,' and it comes from that night in the hotel room when I was nine."

It may offer comfort to some little sisters who are still battling against the nicknames that have haunted them for years, that there are some people who have never been given a nickname—bad or good. They sometimes envy the attention that *any* nickname seems to bestow.

More About Nicknames

A problem with these descriptive nicknames, of course . . .
was that we often believed them.

❧

Another category of slur was sometimes heaped upon our young minds and maligned our brain function. "Numbskull," "Dope," and "Birdbrain" were only the beginning. I was called "Chatterbox" (a Norwegian thing again). But you get the idea. These nicknames can send an unflattering message to us little sisters that is received loud and clear. Along with the labels, we also were the occasional targets of insulting phrases that our siblings brought home from school, such as, "When God passed out brains, you got overlooked." Don't you wonder if they really meant any of this stuff or if they simply enjoyed the hilarious laughter they indulged in when they heard themselves making the jokes? The idea of them enjoying their performances makes me wonder if maybe, for many of us little sisters, we were simply in the wrong place at the wrong time.

Nancy is the youngest of three girls, has a Ph.D. in English, and teaches at a small liberal arts college. She said that it wasn't until her late teen years that it occurred to her that she wasn't stupid. "That's what I was called by my sisters, so that's what I thought I was." A problem with these descriptive nicknames, of course, as Nancy illustrates, was that we often believed them. If the names felt like a taunt, we may have thrown them right back at our siblings, but we couldn't deny that the older siblings, in their cleverness, had used the names first on us. And if it stung us to be called something insulting, there may have been a reason. Maybe a negative name cast doubt on something we'd feared about ourselves: bean pole, fatso, four eyes, shorty, or a myriad of other slightly mean names.

And even if we didn't think the description was honest, maybe we carried the fear, at least for a little while, that we deserved whatever was coming our way. The reason for our accepting that there may have been some truth to the nickname was probably related to our being last in the family and assuming for a long time that we knew the least. (We held that assumption because it was true at the time.) Little sisters who were instructed or told what to do were ripe for believing what they were told, and they were vulnerable to comments from others. In addition to whatever gullibility syndromes little sisters may have carried, it seems to be human nature, too, to believe what we are told. We humans are capable of skepticism, but we exercise it on a relatively small percentage of things said to us.

Another way to think about the comments and nicknames that were thrown our way is to consider the act of labeling that we all underwent. At first the descriptors came exclusively from fact or opinion: girl, daughter, little sister, pest. Then we started to earn some titles through our actions. Maybe we colored things or splashed in the wading pool or dressed up in funny clothes, and people were suddenly calling us artists or swimmers or comics. Sometimes nicknames came from early skills or by accident. Maybe we performed an admirable deed (hitting a triple in a softball game, making a three-point shot during a backyard game of basketball, performing exquisitely at a recital), and we were dubbed "Slugger," "Jump," or "Star." That sort of nickname is something that could drive us for years, and we began to realize that we could do things that would prompt people to call us names that made us feel good.

All through life we're given labels from the outside (taxpayer, traveler, victim, member of the middle class) which may or may not feel as if they describe very much of who we are. But meanwhile, we choose activities and beliefs that bring more meaningful names to us: musician, lifeguard, Buddhist, gardener, teacher, activist. These earned labels that we select and pursue grant us self-esteem that reflects our value to the world. Nicknames and labels may make us feel annoyed or they may make us feel special; they may come from mischievous siblings, from odd moments with friends, from our biggest fans, or from the world at large. Some of them are out of our control, but others are totally within our own design. We are always free at one particular moment to name ourselves: "Hello, I'm Jane Doe, and I'm a . . .

. . . marathon runner."

. . . computer programmer."

. . . soprano."

. . . librarian."

. . . surgeon."

. . . reporter."

. . . weaver."

. . . fan of Wagnerian opera."

We can fill in those blanks with whatever we want and whatever we take pride in, whether or not it earns us money. As we remember that the nicknaming of us by siblings was often a thoughtless whim in childhood, we can appreciate that the labeling and naming of ourselves in adulthood is a privilege that we can indulge in with gusto and pleasure.

The Unwanted Kid—Us?

The insults leveled at us as children often stick much harder and longer than our siblings imagine they will.

❧

Another painful insult from siblings went right to our biggest fear about being the last baby in the family. Was there any affront more tormenting than: "Mom never wanted you anyway. I heard her say so," or "You were adopted!" What desolating words to fall on our young and tender ears—our worst fears brought to light. We were an accident of some sort or other—an unwanted branch on the family tree. Our struggle for love was then compounded. Not only did we have to wheedle some of the love away from what was being offered to the older siblings, we had to persuade our parents that we were worthy of any love in the first place, or so we thought.

Hillary recounts the story of the closest in age of her three older sisters, who "did not want to be associated with me; it was hurtful. She wanted to be associated with the older ones. She pushed me away. She said to our mother one day, 'You know, it was really better when there were just three of us.'" If that kind of comment doesn't set a little kid back five spaces, I don't know what would. As an adult—albeit a happy one with wide personal interests and a wonderful family—Hillary says, "I still want to be included." Perhaps her sister's attitude was fed by the fact that she was four years old when Hillary was born, so the attention the sister had received from the oldest sisters undoubtedly shifted when Hillary came along.

The insults leveled at us as children often stick much harder and longer than our siblings imagine they will. There we were, stressed out by these barbs of inferiority slung at us by insensitive siblings, and there they were, kids not much older than ourselves just out to have a little fun.

Yet, it's little wonder, isn't it, that we little sisters get cowed sometimes? We are intimidated into feeling like the lesser person. If our next oldest sibling (and all the siblings born after the first one) received some of the same treatment—and no doubt they did—they also had a chance to wear the other shoe and taunt the latest arrival once we were old enough for teasing. Alas.

The Smothered Little Sister

There are some wonderful benefits to a lot of attention, but the time comes for most little sisters when being pampered begins to feel like being hampered.

The opposite of fearing we may not have been wanted is realizing that we were wanted excessively. It is not uncommon for little sisters to be pampered for a while, especially if they have substantially older siblings. The pampering begins as a natural way to deal with the new baby in the house. Everyone wants to participate in cuddling and coddling the smallest member of the family. In some families, however, the coddling becomes a habit that the parents and/or older siblings grow way too accustomed to, and it goes on for years. Being catered to or protected is a condition that a lot of little sisters have to tolerate for much of their childhood. There are some wonderful benefits to a lot of attention, but the time comes for most little sisters when being pampered begins to feel like being hampered. Little sisters quickly learn that being overprotected—even with the kindest of intentions—conflicts with efforts to exercise independence. Sometimes such close attention is a strong inspiration for moving out of the family home and beginning life on our own. Making this break is often challenging; for the overprotected, the move can sometimes take years and can cause a strain in family relations.

Betsy enjoyed a comfortable childhood. As the youngest of several children, she was "protected" by all of her older siblings and her parents. As the older children left the home, she felt that her parents' cumulative concern for all of their children became more and more focused on her as "the baby" of the family. When it was time to go to college, she embraced the opportunity to get out of the spotlight of her family's concerns for her. She recalls, "They could not think of me as anything but the baby of the family, unable to take care of myself." When it was time to get a job, she found one that allowed her to travel to many foreign countries and exercise a lot of independence. She also moved to New York, where her employer's home base was located. However, her parents and older siblings were concerned about her travel and her life in New York, the "dangerous big city." Betsy found that her family's concern was intensified when any of them came to visit her. Eventually, Betsy found that it made her relationship with her family easier if she went to them instead of them visiting her. This kind of solution has more to do with avoiding the problem than tackling it head on, but sometimes avoidance can be a functional and efficient answer. (There are plenty of things in the world that we choose to avoid in order to improve our lives.)

When we little sisters grow into our thirties and forties, and our parents are still reluctant to treat us as adults, finding ways to maintain our adult selves in their presence gives us a sense of control in a situation, which, at that age, we deserve. Betsy doesn't begrudge her parents their attitude; she's learned that they can't be educated out of it, so the solution is to work around it in ways that satisfy all parties.

The "Not Enough" Syndrome

The bonus, of course, is that each time we add another thread of competence to our knowledge base, our self-esteem moves up another notch.

❧

Remember being haunted by the "Ghost of Inadequacy"? Surely, in our adult lives, we find ways to conquer it, but as children, the repeated warnings became a chorus that we heard again and again:

> "You're not old enough . . . to go downtown with out an adult."
>
> "You're not big enough . . . to go up in the tree with the other kids."
>
> "You're not tall enough . . . to get on the Super-Duper ride at the amusement park."
>
> "You don't swim well enough . . . to go canoeing with friends."
>
> "You're not experienced enough . . . to use a power tool."

Did you wonder if it would ever end?

Sometimes the overprotection that some of us felt from parents reinforced the idea that we weren't ready for life. Repeated warnings that began early and followed us year after year—depending upon our requests and upon how protective our parents actually were—gave us a feeling of being held back from what we wanted to do.

Such treatment caused us to be eager participants when opportunities were finally available. We often took these plunges while hearing a small voice in the background wondering if things would work out. Some of us pushed ourselves into risk taking with more energy than we should have. No wonder lastborn children are not only more rebellious, but also more likely to take risks. The two characteristics fit neatly together.

Another aspect of these warnings about inadequacy that often carries into adulthood, is the sense of lack of preparation—the "not enough" syndrome. How do we little sisters handle that? Usually head on. We try to learn as much as we can in the few waking hours available to us each day; some of us go after this learning mania with a vengeance. We are determined to catch up.

Catching up might mean keeping up with the news, with trends regarding our work, with the stock market, with whatever area we want to feel adequate in. It may also mean learning how to be self-sufficient. I have a deep hunch that, more than other types of siblings, little sisters are the biggest enrollees in "Car and Oil Change," "Herbal Alternatives," and "Grouting for Beginners" classes. I suspect we, more than others, pay our hard-earned dollars for magazines, books, and tapes that help us find our way through the world. We're willing to explore virtually anything that promises enough knowledge to certify ourselves as adequate.

Since one of the most important aspects of self-esteem is a sense of accomplishment, doing something well is a grand thing. We all know these things don't have to be public events; rather, they are often the things we do routinely: the special things we do that enhance our relationships and homes, that help us feel part of our community, that make us efficient and competent in our jobs, and that give us satisfaction in our lives. As we appreciate these accumulating capabilities in adulthood, we can still recall (and empathize with currently young little sisters) some of the obstacles that appeared in front of us when we were trying to practice these self-esteem-granting activities.

The bonus, of course, is that each time we add another thread of competence to our knowledge base, our self-esteem moves up another notch. Some little sisters have to remind themselves that a large percentage of self-esteem is under one's own control. We can expand our abilities and our areas of expertise and our personal accomplishments at will, and everything adds up to greater confidence and comfort as adult women.

We Are Well Liked

Lucille Forer believes that most last children, which includes us, have two of the assets of only children— achievement and popularity—without the anxiety that plagues our older brothers and sisters.

❧

Some of the attributes we gained by virtue of being little sisters end up giving us influence in the larger adult world that we would not anticipate. Walter Toman, who was a clinical psychologist at the University of Erlangen-Nurnberg in Germany and whose 1961 book *Family Constellation* was a hallmark in birth order and personality development, claims that little sisters with older brothers attract men easily: "quietly, though, or at least without much ado." He also describes these little sisters as being everything a man would conventionally desire: friendly, feminine, sensitive, warm, sympathetic, and usually tactful, she is also a pal.[7] I have to add that this list of characteristics would also be an attraction for many women when they think about what they value in friends.

Lucille Forer believes that most last children, which includes us, have two of the assets of only children— achievement and popularity—without the anxiety that plagues our older brothers and sisters. In fact, research studies also found that us youngest ones are the most comfortable talking with both peers and adults,[8] no doubt from the practice we had starting from day one. I know you're thinking about how shy you were, but often shyness and openness can coexist in the same person—context can change everything for many of us. We last children have the company of both our siblings and their friends, or if they all go away somewhere, we may have more attention from a parent.

Although some little sisters feel we received the short end of the stick when we were children, a few of the difficulties we experienced turned out to work in our favor. If we had to work harder to be sociable and learn how to have conversations with visitors, the reward was apparently an ease with people that made us well liked later on. Being liked can be a nice boost to a positive sense of self. It's certainly nothing to complain about.

However, we can complain about and wonder why we little sisters with big brothers felt worse about ourselves. Psychologist William Altus, who taught at the University of California at Santa Barbara, learned in a 1976 study that little sisters with older brothers check off more negative adjectives about themselves on a list of descriptive attributes than do little sisters with older sisters. So the study indicates that little sisters of brothers have lower self-esteem than little sisters of sisters.[9] Speculation is in order here. I don't know of research that claims sister/sister sets to be closer or farther apart than sister/brother sets. But it is certainly true that little sisters of sisters often have an opportunity to be apprentices to their big sisters in ways that little sisters and big brothers don't have. If such a relationship is encouraged by the big sister through her sharing of belongings or demonstrating girl stuff, a little sister may have the opportunity to echo the self-esteem of her older sister. Such little sisters may feel nurtured into their next phase of growth, and feel confident about their place in the family. Lisa says her older sister "was like a best friend who was there all the time." Nevertheless, there were certain rules for Lisa as a little sister: "One, never being allowed to sit in the front seat of the car, unless Mom was in a bad mood and neither of us wanted to sit up front—then I had to. Two, never having dolls, stuffed animals, or clothes that were better than my sister's. Three, always getting things last—if we both subscribed to a magazine, I'd have to wait until she was done reading it. Four, always getting hand-me-downs, but since her clothes were always better than mine—or so I thought—I loved them."

But Lisa talks of a big advantage she felt in having an

older sister: "having the trouble paths paved for you." Lisa benefited from having an older sister to set the model of behavior in the house. "As my sister hit her teen years, my parents faced new obstacles of curfews, boys, et cetera. When I got to that stage, my parents were more lenient, they'd been through it with her." Katherine, too, credits her older sister with easing her own growing-up years. "We'd talk about family stuff and help each other sort it all out. We'd stay up late at night talking everything over. We even developed our own sign language, so we could talk to each other across the cafeteria at school, and no one else knew what we were saying." This trail-blazing advantage seems to be more evident for little sisters of sisters or little sisters of both brothers and sisters, than for little sisters of brothers. Lisa and Katherine are clearly little sisters who were very happy to grow up with a big sister in the house. It happens that way plenty of times.

About those brothers. We have to recognize that a double standard was—or is—still active in many of the homes we grew up in. Parents fear less for their sons in all kinds of ways: the potential for physical danger, handling a car breakdown, getting a damaged reputation, even the choice of friends. Parents are often more relaxed about these issues with their sons than with their daughters. When the daughters are younger, this attitude of tolerance gets lumped into the perceived privileges that older siblings receive anyway, and little sisters may feel extra deprived. This gap of independence may increase the difficulty of bonding between brothers and sisters; activities that parallel the girl stuff between many older and younger sisters are less frequent between brothers and sisters. When the cross-sex siblings do play something together, the activities are often in the realm of what interests the big brother, which may or may not interest the little sister. Some athletics and killer computer games still engage more males in our culture. (It should be added, though, that sometimes the interests of opposite-sex older siblings are particularly engrossing to little sisters. In such a case, little sisters are fortunate to have their interests tapped.)

For the most part, the activities we share with our sisters are leading us toward the same place they're headed: female adulthood. But even when little sisters of big brothers share some activities with them, the bottom line is that it is impossible to become what our brothers are going to become: male adults. This difference in sex doesn't mean that sisters and brothers can't be as close or closer than many sisters with sisters. But it seems not too surprising to imagine that the difference often does dictate a childhood for little sisters of brothers that is appreciably different from a childhood of little sisters of sisters.

In addition to little sisters with brothers tending to feel worse about themselves, William Altus's study shows other bad news. The little sisters of brothers marked more negative adjectives to describe their fathers and brothers. These negative feelings apparently tend to spread to their attitudes about men in general.[10] Although the study is more than twenty years old, it was done when some of you reading these words were becoming mature. The extent to which the findings are time-bound is a mystery.

Boosts from Big Brothers

"I got a lot of self-esteem from being good at the sports my brother taught me to play."

Like other little sisters, I was sometimes a pest to my brother (are you surprised?) when we were small. And, like other big brothers, he sometimes accommodated me. As children—in the pre-Star Wars era—the Lone Ranger and Hopalong Cassidy were our heroes. On those days that I was allowed to play with Jerry and his friends— which happened because my girlfriend lived two blocks away and at age four or five I was not always allowed to go to her house—Jerry was Gene Autrey and I was Tateeta, his "Indian helper." I learned years later that Jerry had invented Tateeta so I could play along, which was awfully sporting of him. During play, it was often the case that I was left on the porch to "guard it" while the bigger boys ran through the neighborhood on their exploits, but being part of his inner circle in even a diminished role made me feel good.

Christine also remembers her older brother as a playmate. "When the bane of my existence was being forced to play softball at every recess in grade school—I was terrible, and horribly self-conscious—he would take me outside and pitch balls to me for hours to improve my batting abilities."

Amy, too, says her brother played ball. "I was always such a klutz—a bookworm instead of an athlete. But any of the sports I played with my brother I got good at because he was five years older. In seventh grade gym class, on the very first day of basketball, I did a breakaway lay-up—and made it!—only because I had practiced it with my brother. That was one of two shining moments in gym class. The other one was in Ping-Pong. Our parents gave us a Ping-Pong table when I was about eleven, and my brother and I spent hours at it. I enjoyed the benefits right into college when I was in a table tennis tournament. I teamed up with my boyfriend for pairs, and we were the ones to beat. I got a lot of self-esteem from being good at the sports my brother taught me to play."

Getting these boosts from our big brothers were worth a whole lot more than just the fun of the moment.

What's a Parent to Do?

No one can claim that it's easy to be a parent. Parents have to make a zillion decisions—many in two seconds or less.

❧

It is important to recognize the challenges facing the parents of little sisters and how the responses to those challenges affected us. First of all, before we little sisters were even an imagined part of the family, all of our big brothers and sisters were born. They were born, they grew, they did all the things babies and toddlers and little kids do. And our parents coped and learned, over and over. Then we came along. The last kid in the family. By this time, some parents were pooped out. Little wonder. In this situation, some last daughters receive a great deal of rearing from older sibs. And when the siblings are substantially older, a bond that is rather parental can develop, as it did with Peggy, whose oldest sister is eighteen years older than her.

But another scenario is that as the last issue of our parents, we were clung to, safeguarded, sheltered, and watched like eggs in an incubator. Some parents don't want their families to end, so to speak. They don't like having the children leave the nest, and as each one departs, pressures mount increasingly on us, the last one. This type of family life leads to some last daughters staying very close—geographically as well as emotionally—to their parents. Barbara's life is an extreme example. Barbara's opportunities for what we think of as a full life, with a circle of friends and family plus options to explore a career or vocation, shrank away year by year as she was growing up. Her four older siblings (who were older by rather large gaps) left home, and she stayed on and on. Now she tends to ailing parents with an uncommon grace. She enjoys her siblings' gratitude and accepts the responsibilities that have fallen to her with dignity. Her quiet accomplishments may not be what many people aspire to, but her life emulates a devotion that we can't help but admire.

Let's examine the presumption that most parents want to raise their last daughters with as much fairness as they raised their other children—and that's a presumption that seems too sensible to disagree with. It is interesting to look at some of the dynamics of children in their early years, and think about the impact of parents' roles and responsibilities on children's happiness and growth. For instance, sometimes we last and smallest children needed to be protected from our siblings. The older kids can easily get the upper hand in many situations, and while they may often choose to maintain a fair balance of play, not all big brothers and big sisters play fair all the time. We little sisters may be able to cope with most of our tangles, but sometimes we need intervention. Sometimes we absolutely need protection. The next question, though, is how to judge when protection becomes overprotection? When are parents too eager to interrupt us in the natural competitions and social mischief that siblings inevitably engage in?

No one can claim that it's easy to be a parent. Parents have to make a zillion decisions—many in two seconds or less. We little sisters have to be sympathetic to that difficulty. But the good news is that there is help available for parents of little sisters. Researcher Forer compiled a list of suggestions for parents of youngest children. If parents examine these ideas when they think about the kind of parenting they want to do, their last daughters will be very appreciative, both in the short and the long run.

Suggestions from Forer for raising youngest children:

1. *Make sure the youngest one is not dominated by older siblings.*

Domination means more than physical control. Older siblings should not be permitted to boss or manage their little sisters all the time. And the oldest kids should not always be able to make choices about family activities. Some interests of little sisters will probably be the same interests that the older sibs have already abandoned, but that doesn't mean the family can't experience things again on behalf of the youngest.

2. *Keep teasing by older siblings within careful bounds.*

Give clear limits to the older siblings (out of earshot of the younger ones) about teasing that you overhear. Name calling or insults about little sisters should be kept within the territory of harmless joking. Offer the older siblings the responsibility for demonstrating how to be more mature. Teasing fairly is a good skill for them to learn; it's a social skill that many adults use to interrupt tension or breakdown the formality of a moment. Besides, fair teasing can be a source of fun for kids.

3. *Provide the same opportunity and encouragement for the accomplishments and achievements of your youngest child.*

Support the interests of little sisters through lessons or clubs or extracurricular activities. Be as active a parent for her hobbies and dreams as you have been for your older children.

4. *Stress experiences that lead to self-reliance and self-direction.*

Because she is the youngest and often gets the smallest amount of responsibility, encourage activities such as volunteering for groups where everyone, including little sisters, are strongly valued and given responsibility. At home, allow her to take care of herself for an evening when she insists she's old enough to do so. Ask her to be responsible for dinner once a week, or, when she's older, request that she run errands for you.

5. *Encourage decision making and independence.*

To show her that she can make decisions on her own and needn't rely on older family members, start early to let your youngest have a say in things that affect her— how her room is arranged, which clothes to buy, some choices in menu selections (balanced with the choices of others in the household). When she's older, if she asks you about a dilemma she's having, help her work through the steps to reach a conclusion rather than telling her what to do. Ask her to make decisions that affect other people in the house, and then take her advice. Expect her—don't just encourage her—to exercise independence.

6. *Watch that the youngest does not tackle situations over* *his or her head, as repeated failure will lead to feelings of inadequacy.*

Because the youngest sees many examples of other people doing things better than she does, make sure that she has a peer group to play with so that she isn't constantly trying to keep up with the activities and abilities of older siblings. If she shows interest in something beyond her skills, provide ideas and support for an experience that bridges her current competence with the goal she's aiming for.

7. If there is a special problem, such as illness or loss of a parent, don't forget the needs of the youngest while providing outside help if necessary.[11]

Such help may be valuable and ease emotional distress even if no serious symptoms seem to be present. Family counseling for all members of a family is extremely important, and the blitheful spirits of young children should not dissuade you from helping them through the pain that they're trying to understand.

I like the soundness of Forer's suggestions—teasing within boundaries, offering opportunities to achieve, encouraging decision making, and providing support for serious problems. Little sisters would respond well to parents who followed this list. In many respects, the ideas echo what we think of as good parenting practices. An addendum to the list is the suggestion to beware of double standards for behavior, either by age or by sex.

Parenting is an incredibly complex task; no one who's been through it would disagree. Parents of little sisters simply have a few more points to keep in mind.

On Our Own

Despite the obstacles that little sisters must overcome in their role as the youngest girl, there is surprisingly good news in that when we go out on our own, we often find that we manage as well as—or better than—the next person. The fact is that once we're on our own we learn rather quickly that we are fully capable of negotiating adulthood. What we had expected was that—as in childhood, where everyone older did things better than we did—the adult world would be filled with people who'd gotten there first and were doing an outstanding job. Instead what we discover is that, while some people make terrific adults, lots of people aren't very good at it. We can hold our own just fine.

The bonus for little sisters here is that in those areas

where we're inadequate, we can recognize that fact and pursue steps to correct the condition. Seen in this light, our shortcomings can be viewed as tools for improvement. Nothing is beyond our ability, if we can muster the ambition, time, and funds to conquer it. (Sometimes, it's only a little bit of time and no money; other times it's simply the ambition, and so on. The list isn't as daunting as it first appears.) So the sense of inadequacy we struggled with when we were small can become, for us, the ability to turn a handicap into an advantage.

Another of our abilities is, of course, adaptability. The word *adaptability* may suggest lichens struggling to survive in the tundra or tall men tucked into tiny cars, but it's simply about coping with a good attitude and striving onward. Little sisters are highly capable of adapting. As far as Darwin was concerned, adaptation concerned modifying oneself to fit into the environment and knowing how to accommodate oneself to diversified surroundings when necesssary.[12] Except for those little sisters who are pampered through every whim and desire, the usual pattern of little sisterhood is for us last and smallest ones to expect to be bumped into the smallest space at the restaurant, to make do with the hand-me-downs, or to tolerate the cooler under our feet in the back seat during family trips. Our middle names were *adaptable.* In adulthood, many of us find this particular capability to be a strength.

Some of us little sisters take adaptability too far when we stay in abusive relationships longer than older sisters. Perhaps this tendency is not too surprising when you stop to think about it. If, when we were growing up, we found that love was a mix of affection and excessive harassment, how would we understand how to look for something else as adults? Another reason for this behavior may be our belief in being able to fix things, or perhaps we think we can wait it out. Learning appropriate boundaries and tolerance levels is one task for little sisters as we grow up.

In everyday situations, the adaptability of us little sisters and our inclination to be easy going is exemplary. Traffic jams, inept service, stalled elevator. We're not likely to have cardiac arrest over these problems, like the more anxious firstborn. We can become highly vocal if we're missing the opening number at the Academy Awards or the business appointment we've been anticipating for three months, but in the course of daily life, we generally tolerate these obstacles and alter our schedules. We balance our checkbooks; we sympathize with the clerk; we strike up a conversation with strangers. Life can generally be rearranged. At home, we can do the same. Power outage? Car breaks down? Refrigerator on the fritz? We may throw a small fuss, then we get out the candles, call a cab, and keep the food cold as long as possible. We can figure it out. (Yes, we can be stubborn as large rocks, too. Look at it this way: we're blessed with many attributes; when we're overwhelmed by one of them and not liking the way it feels, we can take a step back, consider other options, and move into a different mode—each situation calls for its own appropriate reaction.) Adaptability is one of our very useful assets. How useful? Darwin says it's the adapters who survive.

CHAPTER THREE

The Competition Game

Dottie [older sister]: I love you.
Kit [little sister]: Really?!

– A LEAGUE OF THEIR OWN –

The idea of competition conjures up a range of connotations in our culture. We may think first of sports—from professional athletics and its surrounding money and media attention to the Olympics and the good will surrounding the heart-warming triumphs of international contenders. Competition also brings to mind politics and the ways that candidates campaign for office—not always a pretty picture. We also think about products, brand names, and how marketing strategies compete to gain our loyalty. Television programs, films, and musical performers vie for our time and our dollars. They compete with each other through advertising and product development.

Competition, we're told in a free enterprise nation, leads to better products and a better life. It's practically a creed.

The nuances of competition influence our lives on a daily basis. Consider the supply and demand rule in economics. Everything from getting a seat on the subway or bus to finding fresh artichokes at the grocer's is hinged on how much is available and how many of us want it.

Competition has a bad reputation in some circles. It can be seen as the evil twin of cooperation. Some people would like to discard competition entirely. But the bottom line is that there are finite resources to distribute. Even if the distribution is done cooperatively, it must be said that those who want the resources inevitably compete for them.

But where are little sisters in this array of definitions? We have to pluck the word competition from its lofty place and market usage and move it down to a personal level. Then we can begin thinking about it in terms of little sisters. Little sisters and their siblings participate in different types of competition—consciously and unconsciously. What are we competing for? Mainly, the love and attention all children need. And supply and demand definitely plays a part.

Competition in Families

Adapting to available resources when we were kids no doubt influenced our later lifestyles and choices.

❧

Most of the little sisters I spoke with remembered some sort of competition with their siblings. Many of us competed physically—trying (usually in vain) to best our older brothers in "gotcha last" games: hitting or tapping him, then running madly to the other end of the house. (Who doesn't recall playing this game in the car! Talk about shooting fish in a barrel.) Or we competed intellectually—trying to measure up to our big sister's grades or awards.

When we didn't win by using obvious techniques, including the ones we saw our siblings use, we grew crafty and clever, we manipulated our parents so we could get what we wanted, or we relied on that age-old tactic: tattling. We little sisters have had to cope with the age and size disadvantage by winning in other ways. Masters—or mistresses—of subversion, we insisted on getting our share of the pie, too, and we discovered and created lots of ways to do it.

A family lives in a particular amount of space, earns a finite amount of money, and has the same amount of time each day. How are those resources divided? Who gets what and how much? In examining this topic, for me the question of who got the biggest bedroom and why raises its ugly head again. (My mother admits to being a *tad* overprotective.) But on a smaller and more universal level, for many of us this disbursement issue can immediately conjure up memories of dividing a treat. Unless it was a Hershey Bar™ with those scored lines, there was no such thing as dividing a candy bar evenly, and cutting the last portion of rhubarb pie in two required geometric calculations for true accuracy; somebody always got the greater, and somebody always got the lesser. If you had fair-minded parents with decent memories in the room, the kids took turns getting the lion's share.

Adapting to available resources when we were kids no doubt influenced our later lifestyles and choices: how we spend our money, our time, our talents, and our mental abilities. Sometimes deprived childhoods lead to extravagant adulthoods. Other times, penurious early years lead to at least cautious if not miserly adulthoods. And occasionally, childhoods filled with every comfort and amenity lead to adulthoods of meaningful but low-paying work.

So there's no simple way to say exactly how resource allotments made during our childhoods will influence us in adulthood. It's useful, though, to recognize that each of us was born into a family where those resource deci-sions were made. We couldn't help but be affected by them personally and by the way we observed the re-sponses of others.

Lessons Learned

Of course, while we're learning to wait for our turn—on the swing, at the computer, hosing down the car—we also learn patience.

❦

One lesson that all kids take away from the process of dividing resources is a good one: Life is not fair. The earlier learned, the better, yes? Having learned it, though, we little sisters didn't simply expect the short end of the stick at every turn; instead, we learned that small victories mattered and that over the long haul, dogged determina-tion was often the only way to achieve our goals. This truism, of course, applies not only to little sisters, but I wonder if little sisters understand it earlier than older siblings, oldest ones in particular?

Another social lesson that we learn in our families is taking turns. My parents have a tape recording they made of Jerry and me when I was two or three and Jerry was six or seven. It was one of those events when parents try to get their kids to say something, and the kid—me, in this case—would have none of it. The questions were easy, like saying people's names and such, but I was apparently not in the mood. What's fun about the tape is that even though Jerry had already had a turn at showing how smart he was, he can be heard in the background, eagerly answering my questions, while my dad is trying to keep him quiet so that I could speak. I finally said some silly talk—a sign of embarrassment? I was very shy as a child and my brother was Mr. Bounce-off-the-Walls, and all of these personality quirks, plus the challenge of learning how to take turns, are revealed on the tape.

My husband, the oldest of four, grew up on a farm, so if he wanted someone to play with, his sister was his only choice much of the time. He remembers taking turns in their play. He says, "If I wanted her to play war with my plastic army men for an hour, I had to agree to play house with her for an hour afterwards." Tit for tat.

Of course, while we're learning to wait for our turn—on the swing, at the computer, hosing down the car—we also learn patience. These are situations where competition teaches us how to cooperate: If we don't let X have a turn, we won't get one ourselves. We also learn the importance of staying in line—no matter how short or long the line is—which helps us learn persistence. Determination is another characteristic that helps us get what we want; it goes along with persistence. Lastly, we painfully come to the understanding that sometimes things work out fairly and sometimes they don't.

Solo Little Sisters

*Subtle and blatant competition is simply
a part of being alive.*

Competition may be a natural part of sibling relationships for most of us, but for those siblings with huge age gaps between them, its role is greatly diminished.

Lynda doesn't remember any quarrels in her home when she was growing up. Her sister and brother were eleven and twelve years older than she was. "No sibling rivalry for me. I never learned how to do any battling, and now I'm not always that easy to get along with." She wonders if sibling rivalry doesn't teach you some skills that she didn't get. "I can be difficult sometimes because I want things to be the way I want them to be." (Tales like Lynda's make us rethink our desire to whine about sibling competition in our own families.)

Beyond the competition that we might or might not experience with siblings, subtle competition is simply a part of being alive. Even if we felt no explicit competition with a sibling, we probably had to compete for Dad's or Mom's attention; they had jobs, home responsibilities, church or social activities, and hobbies. Once we're out in the world, we're pitted into the competitive mode in school and at play, and then later in jobs, in stores, parking lots, movie lines, etcetera, etcetera. Competition is part of the social pattern of our lives.

A Darwinian Looks at Us

Thus, in a climate of limited resources, siblings create unique niches for themselves in order to gain what they need.

Considering the role of competition in the broad context of what we do in the interest of survival leads us to the ideas of Charles Darwin and, specifically, to his studies on how species adapt to change in order to survive. A relevant parallel between the activities of species and families has been described by Frank Sulloway. Sulloway is a Research Scholar at Massachusetts Institute of Technology and has studied and written about the work of Darwin for many years. In his most recent book, *Born to Rebel,* Sulloway links birth order influence to the ideas of Darwin. Sulloway believes that families develop in a manner that echoes Darwin's evolutionary theory. Thus, in a climate of limited resources, siblings create unique niches for themselves in order to gain what they need. Sulloway's theory extends Adler's idea that the family environment is altered each time a new child enters the scene: Each additional child develops uniqueness in order to gain affection and attention.[1]

To learn more about the uniqueness of laterborn children, Sulloway explores research that had been done with people who were not firstborns. He examined information on about 6,500 famous people throughout history; about 650 of them were female. His results echo some things well established by others, including the fact that the firstborns generally agree with the status quo to a higher degree than laterborns. Laterborns are more attracted to innovations and revolutionary ideas when the inventions and ideas are still fresh and unestablished.[2]

Sulloway also introduces a novel idea about gender and birth order. He claims that birth order has a major effect on personality characteristics that are usually associated with sex. Specifically, he says that birth order has two-thirds the influence on the development of gender traits as a person's sex has. So traits such as self-confidence, leadership, and self-assertiveness, which are generally associated with masculine personalities, and traits such as affection, flexibility, and cooperation, which are linked to feminine personalities, are actually nurtured or discouraged to a great degree depending upon birth order.[3] I suspect that many of us lastborn sisters find this idea terrifically appealing and provocative. We may have wondered why we weren't more like our sisters or other women we know. Realizing the impact of birth order on our development gives us more ways to understand ourselves.

The major thrust of Sulloway's book is that those who are not born first are more likely both to adopt unconventional thinking and to become involved in movements supported by those new ideas. He focuses on those who were the first to speak out for the American Revolution, abolition, and Darwin's theory of evolution, among others. This theory, this willingness of laterborns to embrace new ideas, is linked to the finding that laterborns tend to be rebellious, a trait adopted in childhood in order to be different from older siblings and to be noticed. Sulloway focuses on all children who weren't born first, though he notes birth order when he knows it. We little sisters are all laterborns, of course, no matter how large the family. With the growing prevalence of small families, many of us who are laterborns are lastborn.

After having learned about this tendency to embrace avant-garde ideas, I was reminded of an event in my early teens, a day in junior high when we had a substitute teacher in geography. He pulled down the world map and explained the theory of plate tectonics by pointing out how the continents, at some point, seemed to have been one giant land mass. He then said the theory wasn't true (because in the early sixties, scientists hadn't accepted it yet). I remember staring at the map and thinking how those points and inlets of land seemed to fit together in a lot of places, and I wanted to believe in this renegade theory. I didn't join a movement to crusade for plate tectonics, but I was happy and proud a few years later when I learned that the theory had been accepted by the scientific community.

Furthermore, I've noticed that much smaller ideas than plate tectonics appeal quickly to me and to my friends who are little sisters. For instance, we like that short rubber tube that you insert garlic cloves into, roll back and forth, and Presto! the skin is shed. We like the idea of Mozart's music providing psychological benefits beyond the pleasure of the music. We like the idea of being in the sun at least twenty minutes per day, and of eating lots more vitamin C than the RDA suggests. And we liked a lot of these things when they were very cautiously suggested as good ideas or sound policies. We like ideas long before they're embraced by our oldest siblings. The older siblings bring skepticism to our eagerness, and often the balance is probably not a bad thing, but it's good we keep pushing the envelope. We keep the wheels of some types of progress (the unconventional, the rebellious) moving ahead.

Finding Our Place in the Family

Each infant coming into a family unknowingly challenges the status quo in order to make as large a niche for itself as it can.

In childhood, it seems that winning takes on many forms, and competition is reflected in many behaviors. So if we little sisters have to compete for love, how do we do it? The easiest way would be to become the loudest kid, the most demanding kid, the most unrelenting kid. Could be. But consider some other ways to think about competition.

A firstborn may find that being loud and obnoxious brings every conceivable favor his or her way. The secondborn may arrive and try to imitate the firstborn, but the firstborn's been at it longer and is much more successful, so the secondborn may experiment with some other tactic, such as being laid-back and relaxed. It works. Fine. That behavior earns sufficient attention and enough love. This child could be a little sister if she was the lastborn, but what if another sister comes along as a thirdborn, and these first two personality types are already taken? She seeks a variation on the theme. Whiner, perhaps. An eager-to-please. A stand-off-er. A cuddle bunny. A hopelessly naughty. A comedy queen. A calmer-downer. A wise counselor. A nonstop complainer. A shy-beyond-words. The possibilities become more varied depending upon the number of children in a family. What we're witnessing here is competition through differentiation.

Humans are wily early in their lives. If not, we wouldn't have survived this long. Consider that we know 20,000 words by the time we reach kindergarten, and well before any of us cares much about words, we're cunningly knowledgeable about body language. Occasional specials on PBS show researchers' films displaying an enormous range of physical responses by three- and four-month-old babies to their mothers' actions. The babies imitate, echo, and beckon. They are highly focused on pleasing the adults around them, and they learn at an incredibly young age how to interpret and respond to the movements and sounds of the words of adults. These early aspects of behavior are the results of the desires for comfort, love, and food. As children learn the dance of interaction with parents and other family members, they're also observing how others interact. They witness how other children get attention, incur anger, or remain on the sidelines. They experiment by imitating and quickly learning to behave differently, because in most situations, the most effective way to get attention is to be different—quiet among the noisy, noisy among the quiet, gentle among the rambunctious, and so on. They differentiate themselves through their actions, which, in the world of birth order, is how they compete. According to Sulloway, each infant coming into a family unknowingly challenges the status quo in order to make as large a niche for itself as it can. And thus they eventually behave in a pattern that suits them, and they come to be described as "the quiet one," "the good one," "the one who acts up," and so on. Therefore, it is competition with our siblings for attention, love, and food that leads us to some of our early personality characteristics.

Mimi attributes her jokester personality to being a little sister with two older sibs. "Growing up, my brother got labeled 'the bad one,' because he was always acting out and upsetting my mom and dad. My sister coped by becoming 'the good one.' She was good at everything she did: a straight-A student, a good athlete. And it left me with a little lost feeling, like I didn't quite know where I fit. So I started to get funny. That's where a lot of my joking around comes from. If I could get a laugh from my dad, it made my day."

Being different works for little sisters in lots of ways. We do it when we're infants to gain attention, love, and food, and we do it when we're older children or teenagers in order not to compete directly with talented siblings. Sometimes our desire to find another playing field is a way of rebelling against what's expected of us; other times we may simply not want to be associated with our siblings or their activities. Fortunately, there is a profusion of activities to be interested in. Such a range of choices makes it relatively easy for us to find the niche of our dreams.

When Competition Serves Us

*Competing successfully meant that each sibling not only
chose a different arena in which to explore,
but also to excel.*

❧

Competition is at work in our lives in several ways. Our first competition was the pattern of behavior that we adopted in order to gain our share of attention, love, and food when we were very young. As we grew older, we were often highly aware of garnering attention through specific actions (completing tasks quickly, adopting a favorite color, developing breakfast preferences different from those of our siblings). There is yet one more permutation of competition to consider, which is a version that blends the first two. This last competition undoubtedly grows out of our early urges to be different from our siblings, but at the same time, it includes a conscious effort to excel. What makes this version of competition somewhat unusual is that all of us siblings are competing, but we're not playing the same game. Not quite.

Ursula, the youngest of three sisters said that her childhood was strongly competitive, "We were always, always competing. We each played an instrument—but a different instrument: The oldest, piano; the middle, clarinet; and me, violin. They hated listening to my violin. They made so much fun of me."

The competition between Ursula and her sisters extended in lots of other directions, including sports and careers. The girls even differentiated themselves in skiing, one choosing Alpine, another downhill, and the third, cross-country. Her sisters' self-interest was most apparent to Ursula when she entered a rebellious phase at seventeen. "I went overboard in everything, in relationships and in trying everything out. I wish my big sisters had told me more about the world or taught me more. There was so much competition among us, at that age that they didn't want to tell me a thing." The positive side of Ursula's family competition is that each of the girls has worked hard to distinguish herself as an adult. One works with horses, one is an environmental biologist, and one is a photographer. For Ursula and her sisters, competing meant working hard to outdo one's self—and one's sisters.

Vanessa and her sister, Erica, who's three years older, experienced a competition that resonates with lots of little sisters, whether we have older sisters or older brothers. Vanessa describes her older sister as being "smart and very accomplished; everything she's done, she's done well. She took ballet, even danced professionally, and did wonderfully, so I never took it. I had to be more creative in what I chose to do, so I wouldn't be involved in things she did." They attended different high schools, which Vanessa appreciated. "It took a while to realize that I could be as smart as my sister. We are now attending the same college, even majoring in the same subject though following very separate interests." Vanessa and Erica now enjoy each other a great deal and are even writing a book together.

Lois J., whose sisters are three and five years older than she is, wrote to me and said that when the sisters recently gathered together, "The same traits came out that have always been there—my oldest sister made sure all was taken care of, my middle sister made sure she got out of the majority of work, and I got by with murder!" (The women are all in their early fifties, by the way.) Sometimes the skills we master are the dynamics of relating to others, which can be powerful tools. Lois J. also reported that she and her sisters love each other dearly and do a good job of tolerating their least favorite qualities in one another.

Laura grew up with one sister who was two years older. "We were always competitive with each other. We purposely had different interests. She was into drama and in plays, so I was on the newspaper. She played in band, so I played in the orchestra. She was a bookworm, and I was a jock." Laura and her sister drove themselves to excel in their chosen activities.

For these sisters, competing successfully meant that each sibling chose a different arena in which to excel. (Competing by being different occurs in the world-at-large, too. Consider the first person to use an oddly-shaped tennis racket or to dance on stage barefooted or to move from naturalistic to impressionistic painting. Experimenting with ways to be different and finding an audience that appreciates you is often an effective way to have an impact on the culture.) Competition of all types seems to have been planted deeply into the sisters' lives, although in some ways it may have limited their participation in activities because of their siblings' prior success in the same activities. On the other hand, the feeling of competition acted as an extra pressure to urge them on to do their best in their own pursuits. Whatever difficulties they faced, the end result worked. Perhaps we little sisters— most of us—have to accept a good dose of competition in our lives as part of the passage to adulthood.

Growing Up Close

Expectedly, researchers also found that little sisters who are closer in years to their brothers and sisters might have more interests in common, play more with each others' friends, miss each other more when separated, and be less likely to want to be rid of each other.

Even though we little sisters often choose different activities as our own proving ground, we sometimes gain benefits from simply being the lastborn child. Statistically, we little sisters with brothers who are between two and four years older do better on tests of verbal meaning and quantification.[4] Similarly, if we have brothers or sisters within a few years, our college entrance exams tend to be higher.[5]

Expectedly, researchers also found that little sisters who are closer in years to their brothers and sisters might have more interests in common, play more with each others' friends, miss each other more when separated, and be less likely to want to be rid of each other.[6] (". . . less likely to want to be rid of each other." How do you suppose they worded the question that prompted that answer?) The findings seem sensible. Siblings who grow up close in age and play together, also learn to rely on each other. I found this closeness to be true for many of the little sisters I spoke with who had siblings who were close in age to themselves, although a few of them said they drifted away from their siblings to a greater or lesser degree in their adult years.

Patricia and her sister, who was twenty-two months older, were good friends when they were youngsters. Patricia remembers sharing a dog, Skippy, with her sister. The three of them would walk to the park where the girls would eat their bologna and Wonder Bread™ sandwiches while sharing bites with Skippy. She remembers, too, when they went to the Disney™ movie *Greyfriars Bobby* (a touching tale based on a true story of a Skye terrier who became a neighborhood pet in Edinburgh in the nineteenth century). There, decked out in their matching outfits—reversible jackets, plaid on one side and navy corduroy on the other—and little hats, they sat close together through the heart-wrenching film. Patricia recalls, "walking up the aisle, hugging each other, and sobbing" over the film's ending. They also played together, just the two of them or with neighborhood friends.

While the girls were close as children, the relationship between Patricia and her sister changed as they grew older. Patricia earned high scores on school assignments, but her sister always acheived slightly higher scores. Patricia never felt as smart as her sister. The two, however, remained close in high school and attended the same college. Once they were finished with college, her sister got a good job with an airline and has been with the same company for decades. Patricia went to graduate school at Columbia University, where she won awards for her poetry. Patricia's temperament and her education led her to adopt a philosophical viewpoint in her opinions, and she was given to quoting lines from her readings to illustrate a point. Her older sister began to refer to her as "my older little sister." The phrase was expressed with the greatest respect, and Patricia felt as though she'd been "given a prize." Her sister continues to honor Patricia's intellectualism. When she and Patricia discuss books they're reading, she will say, "As a lay reader, I found ..." to designate that her opinion is less educated than Patricia's. Although the two women have occasional telephone conversations, they see each other infrequently.

Diana and her sister were also close when they were younger, but found their paths parting even before adulthood. Diana was a mere fourteen months younger than her sister. As teens, they often got into what Diana called "little troubles." She says, "I was in a conspiracy with her—she was my sister! I think there was a bit of worshipping going on." Even while their compatibility was evident, some differences began to surface. "I'm much more introverted," Diana said. "She's very explosive—acts first, thinks later, and the consequences are not considered. I spend a lot of time thinking things through. Sometimes I don't act on things because of considering the possible consequences, which is not always a benefit."

Diana's sister was also jealous. "She's still jealous, over things that are really silly. When we were young she was jealous and thought she was stupid because I got better grades in school. In fact, she did have a harder time than I did, but I was home studying while she was out with her friends. What did she expect?" Diana's sister ended up dropping out of high school but later earned a GED. Diana went on to earn a bachelor's degree and a graduate degree.

Diana reports that she and her sister don't talk frequently any more. They live half a continent apart. She adds, "For years when I was younger, I was more willing to put up with things. I don't feel that I have to do that any longer. I still consider her my friend and sister, but the geography makes it difficult, for us anyway. It's hard to maintain a relationship over the phone."

Laura, who lives on the East Coast, has had similar long silences with her sister. "I saw her last fall; she's in

San Francisco. We had a very nice time, but after that, I didn't hear from her, even though I wrote. I don't understand it totally, but she wants to be left alone."

There seems to be no easy predicter for how our childhood sibling relationships will evolve as we grow into adults. The only thing we can be certain of is that each of us undergoes many changes; the changes may sometimes bring us together, and other times they may lead us apart.

Jumping into the Gene Pool

However, if we bear a strong outwardly physical resemblance to our siblings, it is more likely that we do match up on the insides, too.

When you think about genes, where does your mind take you? For me, I wonder about how much we match other people—not only outside, in the physical things that we can see, but inside, in all of the mysterious places that we can't see. It's remarkable. When I think about genes and siblings, I wonder what aspect of one sibling is an aspect of another sibling as well. Research on siblings has not attracted a lot of attention over the years among the general public. (That's surprising, don't you think, since so many of us are siblings?) Scientists didn't become interested in siblings with earnestness and sincerity, until about a hundred years ago. The first recorded comparisons of siblings were done in the late 1800s by Sir Francis Galton (Galton was Charles Darwin's cousin), who measured the heights of siblings to see how they contrasted.

Scientists since Galton have compared family members in any number of ways. Their findings tell us that, appearance-wise, we are often different from our siblings. This dissimilarity is also true for health matters—if a sibling contracts an ulcer, there is no particular reason to believe that we will, too, and we have an only slightly higher possibility of an organ match with our siblings than with someone in the general population. However, if we bear a strong physical resemblance to our siblings, it is more likely that we match up on the insides, too, all the way through our blood and tissues. Useful information, in case an organ match-up need arises.[7]

While there will be no lectures here on genes, it may be helpful to recall the Austrian monk Gregor Mendel and his work with peas. Like peas, we have the opportunity to inherit things from our parents. Our siblings had the same opportunities.

We are likely to be similar to our siblings to some extent, which can be fabulous, but there are moments when we shudder to claim any amount of similarity. Recalling the way that big brother gingerly took a shovel and lobbed off the head of a harmless garter snake or the ease with which big sister pilfered mother's favorite earrings and recklessly lost them at the beach, we shrink at the idea that we may one day act as they do (if such actions could have a genetic basis).

Even when we aren't thinking scientifically about genes, we little sisters often find ourselves wondering if or how much we're like our siblings. We've been helped along by parents and friends who remind us that we are the little sister of so-and-so brother or sister and that brother or sister is often described as smart with his numbers or good on her French horn or a talented golfer or artist or actor.

Lucy understood this comparison all too well. "One of the biggest things I remember is that I was always preceded by somebody. My oldest brother was captain of the chess team and very intellectual, and my sister was popular and well liked. I remember being introduced as the little sister of so-and-so. I felt short-changed, like I could never enter the world as myself, especially in the small town we grew up in." As soon as Lucy was old enough, she and her guitar moved to Seattle where she played in coffee houses for several years.

Regardless of whatever characteristics we inherited or whatever we were *expected* to inherit, we have to make our way as we can. No surprise there. It's true for everyone. Little sisters, though, may watch talents bloom for older sibs and wonder if they'll be blessed with the same gifts. We have to wait, which is one of the things we're used to anyway.

Tattling, Oh Tattling

So it can be no surprise that one of our primary methods of self protection was tattling.

❧

Remember when we irked our older siblings? The inevitable pay-off was some painful consequence, such as pulled hair, a twisted arm, or being held down with the threat of saliva dripping above us—usually sucked back in the nick of time, thank goodness!

From the viewpoint of our older siblings, we may have appeared as little rascals exercising more power than they were ready to allow us to use. Or perhaps they thought we were trying to get their goat just to prove that we could. They may have thought we were acting spoiled, or they were fed up with us. Whatever the cause, they must have had times when they felt they needed to reassert their status as earlierborn or older or wiser or stronger. Or sometimes they may have had a bad day, and we were around to get the brunt of their frustration.

Regardless of the reason, most little sisters remember some unpleasantness meted out by the older siblings. What was our recourse? Little sisters, as small girls especially, have darn few defenses to rely on. We were smaller, we didn't know as many hiding places, we couldn't throw a pillow or snap a towel with nearly the gusto of the older ones. We had to take advantage of what few tools were available to us. So it can be no surprise that one of our primary methods of self protection was tattling.

Tattling, for us, was a way to respond to the weight of competition when the playing field lost all appearance of being level and we felt ourselves sliding toward disaster. For a few minutes, we may have put up with having our arm twisted if it meant that we could borrow a sweater or win a favor from the older sib. (Sometimes just making a simple request set them off. How were we to know?) But when the moment finally came, when the price went too high, the deal was off, and it was time to tattle. Tattling often meant the end of a particular exchange, and some little sisters felt guilty about blowing the whistle. At the time, however, such drastic measures were, I'm sure, the only option that seemed sensible.

What about the times when our parents stepped out? An absence of adults in the house could cause both an increased bossiness by older siblings and perhaps even an increase of harassment by us little sisters. Risky times. When mom and dad finally returned, the older evil ones could be "told on." Sometimes that brutally honest revelation brought nothing but pure joy—a perfect sense of power, even if it was accompanied by an admonishment that we should behave better, too. Older kids have the burden of setting the good example, so their scolding is usually more severe.

I can recall such an evening. Our parents went somewhere, and, after Jerry and I had a scuffle or two, I decided to keep a list. I opened a notebook on a table in my room, and each time Jerry did anything, I stole to my room and printed it neatly, numbering each infraction. When my parents came home, I turned in my catalog of evidence—"threw pillow at my head," "wouldn't take turns with TV programs," etcetera. He was scolded, which was not an uncommon event for him. And, from my vantage point, the scolding didn't have much of an impact, but it gave me short-term satisfaction.

It must be noted that sometimes, even during the very acts of tyranny, we little sisters could gain control of a sibling situation by uttering those three magic words: "I'm gonna tell." The precise inflection of the words is learned early on, almost by instinct. "I'm gonna tell." It's a mighty phrase, a rising crescendo with a final twist on the last syllable. That short tune offered immense power to us little sisters as we employed one of the few threats we could exercise.

Our impulse to tattle has been imitated in much broader contexts, with some remarkable effects. Consider for a moment the profound effects of tattling on American history: Benedict Arnold was a tattler. John Dean tattled on Nixon. Countless whistle-blowers have tattled on companies engaging in illegal or dangerous practices. In our own homes, we little sisters have foiled many a plan and revealed many a plot. In the big picture, tattling often serves the course of justice. Each of us little sisters, on a lone mission, has played a key role in civilizing the older siblings in our homes. We bore the brunt of being called a tattletale, and we turned them in over and over and over again. Eventually, they took some of the lessons to heart and modified their behavior. We little sisters have to take credit for shaping the actions of many members of society. They arrived at their places in the adult world with many of their evil impulses in check because we did what we could to keep them on the straight and narrow. Even if our immediate goal was to save ourselves, I think little sisters deserve credit for continually keeping the usefulness of tattling in the public mind.

The Next Chapter in the Child-Rearing Manual

Once children gain some sophistication in figuring out who wants what and who's tricking whom, the game's up, and parents have to move on to the next chapter in their child-rearing manual.

❦

Well, we can't think about competition without thinking about the ways parents use it for their own purposes. Maybe their goal is: "Who can clean up their toys first?" or "Who can eat their lima beans first?" The purpose of these competitions is for the parents to extract a particular behavior from a child while camouflaging that behavior in a game that the kids are supposedly playing with each other. If you ponder the setup, you may realize that the basic goal of trying to accomplish something by pitting key players against each other is a plot device used in clever dramas. You've probably seen it time and again. So did our parents. So they tried the same thing. In my house, the game plan was developed by my father. One day Dad announced a competition for piano practicing. Who could practice more in a given month—Jerry or me? The ploy was transparent because Jerry didn't want to take piano lessons, but Dad thought he'd try it anyway.

Our piano was down in the basement, and next to it was the laundry room door. An Allis-Chalmers™ calendar hung on the door. The top half of each month was a seasonal outdoor setting with a bright orange tractor featured prominently; the bottom half displayed the month's numbers on a spacious background. My brother and I were to write down our practice time each day on the calendar, and there was a prize of coins promised to the one who practiced the most by the end of the month. This game ended up teaching me a key element about competition: You can't win if the other team won't play. In fact the game doesn't actually happen. But I didn't know about forfeits yet.

Meanwhile, in the basement, the calendar gained daily scribblings that were mostly in my handwriting. The fact was that my brother had little interest in piano; the competition, which was created to inspire more practicing by him, was not working. Except for a few times when guilt and foul weather drove him to the basement, Jerry wouldn't practice. And a few cents or the opportunity to triumph yet again over his sister, when he already had such a huge quantity of winnings, was simply not appealing enough to draw him into this competition. Thus, I won. But what did I win? Not much. A little money, I guess, but it wasn't bestowed with any pomp or ceremony. (I also improved my piano playing.) The prize, such as it was, had been forfeited to me by the absence of my brother. I received it, but it felt like a win that didn't count; there was no pleasure in it. After that month, I don't recall our parents trying competition as a tool for behavior changes. We had all learned a lesson, though it wasn't the lesson my parents had hoped for.

We know that some of these competitive games work on children. Usually, though, the younger, the better. Once children gain some sophistication in figuring out who wants what and who's tricking whom, the game's up, and parents have to move on to the next chapter in their child-rearing manual.

Summing Up

Competition is a complex aspect of our little sister lives. Initially, it played a key role as we determined behaviors for ourselves and arranged our place in the family. Later it became a major system for the way that many of us interacted with our siblings. In some cases, it worked to benefit us, helping us develop strength of character or doggedness or talents we may not have developed without extra pressure. And we have to admit that sometimes it hindered or discouraged us. But, overall, engaging in competition gave us the opportunity to learn lots of lessons. It gave us practice in dealing with disappointments and in taking turns; it helped us learn patience and determination. Because of it, we sometimes were forced to tattle—for the good of our sibs, of course. Finally, the act of competing gave us practice in negotiating disagreeable situations; such practice would later benefit us in successfully handling a host of adult experiences.

CHAPTER FOUR

Learning the Ropes and Making Our Way

Dedicated to our older siblings who will undoubtedly regard this as just another form of harassment.

– *THE SIBLING,* BRIAN SUTTON-SMITH AND B.G. ROSENBERG –

Ah, mischief—little sister to rebellion. Tricks, jokes, silly little things. Mischief is the polite word for the harmless retaliation that kids love to indulge in. From jumping out of a closet and shouting "Boo!" to creating an elaborate hoax involving maps, chalk signals, arranged rocks, and phony telephone numbers, kids love pulling pranks, and they love it even more when everyone gets a big hoot out of it.

After hearing about "the best trick in the world," children often decide to try it out on siblings. When it works, and especially when it doesn't, children learn more about the personalities of the people they live with, and may learn how much the adults are willing to tolerate from this particular style of make-believe and trickery.

Apprenticing

Lois found herself the victim of her sister's mischief, which is one way to gain instruction even though it's more stressful than being an outside observer.

❧

Playing with our older brothers and sisters is educational in more ways than we can fathom. They set all kinds of examples for us. Among their behaviors, of course, are their personal forms of mischief. We can't help but learn something about how the world works by watching what our siblings do and how everyone reacts. What we see helps us make decisions about the kinds of mischief we may pursue on our own.

Diane's brother, about four years older than her, waited until their mother was out on an errand and then said, "Let's play barber." She agreed because, as with all little sisters, an invitation to play *anything* with big brother was not to be turned down. Even his next sentence didn't cause her to hesitate: "Let me practice on you." And the game began.

"He cut my eyebrows off," she reports. He also poked a hole in her skin, but the game stopped when their mother returned home earlier than expected. "Perhaps she sensed something was up," Diane says. Even though Diane was the victim of her brother's mischief, she learned something about the timing of pranks, in terms of when to do what in order to avoid getting into trouble, and what her mother would and wouldn't approve of—all good lessons.

Margaret was another little sister whose older sibling went after her with a pair of scissors. The older sister was apparently a bit jealous of the curls on little Margaret, who was little enough that her hair had never been cut. The older sister—still a pre-schooler herself—lured Margaret under the kitchen table and snip-snipped those insulting curls off, so that they both had bone straight hair. What a marvelous example of taking control of a situation.

Maeve remembers how mischief was suppressed in her family. She and her middle brother (of five children) often got into trouble together, usually from scuffling. Their skirmishes were generally ignored when they were playing outdoors, but Maeve remembers that when they took long drives for their summer vacations to Canada, her brother had to sit in the front seat of the car with her parents so that the two of them could be kept under control. One can imagine the pent-up tension that this "so near and yet so far" arrangement created.

Lois found herself the victim of her sister's mischief, which is one way to gain instruction even though it's more stressful than being an outside observer. Lois and a friend were sleeping on the porch one warm summer night. "Inside the house, my sisters created a scenario that made it sound as if one of them was getting killed, and the door to the house was locked. My middle sister was scratching on the glass, and the two of them were howling as if they were being brutally murdered." Although it was terrifying at the time, Lois now looks back on the event wryly: "We didn't think to applaud."

Our apprenticeship had several layers. We often served as guinea pigs for our older siblings' mischief. This role seemed fun because we were gullible, and we thought our older siblings would keep our best interests in mind. When our confidence in them was betrayed and we became the victims of sibling mischief ourselves, we learned a lesson in how the world can sometimes work. And we learned more about the power of mischief.

Watching the Masters

*Because of the various models our older brothers and sisters
provided, we were able to learn both
blatant and subtle tactics.*

❧

Dinner often provides a forum for mischief, if not for downright rebellion. Who's kicking whom under the table? Who can successfully roll her beans into her napkin? Who can hide her carrots under the mashed potatoes? And who can slip a treat to Poochie when no one's looking? Food, for many of us little folks, had a much more important role to play than ending hunger; it embodied the opportunity for mischief on its way to rebellion.

My brother performed a specific form of mischief one evening at dinner that proved to be a fabulous benefit to me. I was four, and we were having spinach for dinner. Like many four year olds, spinach didn't appeal to me. It had come out of a can, as most of our vegetables did in those days, and it wasn't a pretty sight. I was a finicky eater who would have been happy to live on raw carrots, hard-boiled eggs, macaroni and cheese, and cold hot dogs. But here we were with a plop of leaky spinach on our plates, and my father was telling us to eat it.

Jerry was getting more pressure to eat the spinach than I was. Perhaps he was fighting it harder, or perhaps he was getting a special invitation to show his little sister how big boys should behave. Whatever the motivation for the pressure, after a certain point, he ate it. And as we all sat there around the table, it came right back out. He vomited the spinach, and whatever else, right back onto his plate—where it had all once been. I remember watching it fill the plate—just up to the edge, not a drop more. What a show! Boy, what great fortune for a little sister— I didn't have to eat a bite of spinach that evening, or any other evening, either. It became vegetable *non grata* in our house—canned spinach was never served again. (He claims, of course, to have done it on purpose. What elegant timing.)

If we can recall some of the innumerable moments of childhood when we saw the successes and failures of our siblings, we realize that each one provided a learning opportunity: "That ploy *was* successful." "Oops, don't try to get away with *that* little prank." And so on. Because of the various models our older brothers and sisters provided, we were able to learn both blatant and subtle tactics. In the process we learned more about our parents, their expectations, and the limits of their tolerance. *Bless* those big sibs!

Co-Conspirators

A door opened for me that day that made me feel linked to my brother in a new way.

❧

The step after apprenticeship is conspiracy. Conspiratorial mischief demanded the involvement of at least two minds. We little sisters became co-conspirators when we did more than take orders: We started contributing ideas.

By virtue of having more experience in the ways of the world, older brothers and sisters were generally more able to concoct and orchestrate the more elaborate mischief. But we little sisters were eager learners, and the fun of conspiracy was a fine catalyst for soaking up all of the experience and wisdom that was offered to us. Beyond the fun was the thrill of being accepted by the big siblings. It was as though we'd passed the ritual torment and had been accepted into the exclusive club of our older sisters or brothers. The "me versus them" dissolved into "us versus the rest of the world."

My own first lesson into group mischief came early. At about age seven, my brother, who was often mischievous when he was young, wanted to try what he thought was a sure thing—an April Fool's trick. (I can imagine his euphoria at discovering that an entire holiday was devoted to mischief.) So he corralled me into secrecy and began organizing a practical joke to play on mom.

Jerry sent me down to the kitchen for a spoon (*he* didn't want to get caught doing anything suspicious), and I can remember slowly sliding the wooden drawer open and lifting the spoon out of the nested stack. I cleverly tucked it under my shirt and snuck back upstairs. In the bathroom, Jerry put the spoon on the floor near my face and had me lie on my stomach near the toilet. Meanwhile, he pried the plastic top off a can of Drano™ and put it on the floor beside me. My role was easy—close my eyes and lie still.

He then raced downstairs and gave a loud, panicked report to my mother about my apparent poisoning and early demise. It worked oh-too-well. Poor mom. The thought of her beloved daughter laid out by Drano™ made her go ballistic. When she ran up the stairs and saw—almost immediately—that we'd played a joke, she was barely comforted. The momentary horror had already sent her over the top, and she gave Jerry a spanking for his ingenuity. I was ignored—thankfully—since I was seen as too little to have possibly conceived the scheme myself. (I recall that my four-year-old mind was a little disappointed that she'd actually believed—if only for a nanosecond—that I was stupid enough to eat Drano™. I liked the way it smelled, but I was no dope; I *knew* it was poison. Oh, well.)

That afternoon was nevertheless filled with lessons for me. I had been taken under the wing of my brother to both plot—through my tacit agreement—and execute a fairly intricate practical joke. I felt that I'd gained his trust as a partner in mischief. And I knew that in the future, he would invite me to participate in his tricks and plans again. A door opened for me that day that made me feel linked to my brother in a new way.

What I didn't realize at the time was that this youthful initiation had seeded my future as a co-conspirator of mischief. That day, Jerry had begun my education in plotting, conspiracy, and courage. What a package. I would draw on these strengths in my later years, of course.

Getting Naughty

When we engage in rebellion, we are aware that someone will probably be unhappy about the act if we get caught.

❧

When we look back at our childhoods and think about the tiny troubles we got into, the friskiness we yielded to, and the impish naughtiness we indulged in, we might say that those years served as our boot camp of sorts, a proving ground. Early mischief prepared us for our forays into conventional rebellion—how to get away with things, how to flout rules and regulations, how to ignore authority figures, and what to do when caught. Oh, the lessons. How valuable they were.

At some point in our lives, those innocent games of early mischief evolved into somewhat less innocent activities of rebellion. The mischief itself seems less important than the intent we used when we undertook the activity. By that I mean that lots of the early mischief seems to be aimed at having fun of some sort. Mischief may be planned, but kids don't do it to get into big trouble generally, and they often are surprised to learn that they pushed parents or other authority figures over the edge. Certainly my brother's Drano™ episode was only plotted to fool mom. Did he imagine her whooping with laughter when she found out it was a trick? Did it occur to him that he might reap the biggest spanking of the year? I don't know.

The leap from mischief to rebellion involves doing exactly what parents tell us not to do—honking the horn one more time, giving the dog one more cookie, jumping on the bed for one more minute ("one more" often seems to be part of the recipe). And doing that "one more" thing *might* lead to a time-out, a lost privilege, or a humiliating scolding. We want to see what happens. Will it be as bad as they say it will? The intention behind our disobedience is close to rebellion, but it's amateurish and misses the nuances of rebellion.

When we engage in rebellion, we are aware that someone will probably be unhappy about the act if we get caught. In fact, we know we're gambling with big trouble. It almost goes without saying that an act is not rebellious unless we've been warned against doing it both by our parents and by their society. Rebellion is a qualitative leap beyond mischief. Therefore, rebellion usually involves willfully and knowingly breaking serious rules. If we're caught, of course we have to pay a price.

My first memory of an act of rebellion—puny as it seems now—was in the fifth grade. I don't mean to claim that I didn't get into trouble when I was younger, but the trouble was often based on misunderstandings or naïveté; basically, I tried to be a good girl. But in the fifth grade, I was very interested in baseball (especially Sandy Koufax) and the World Series, no matter who was playing. At Brookside Elementary School in St. Louis Park, Minnesota, the school officials allowed the students to watch the games on a television in the school auditorium after we finished eating lunch. I don't remember any of the particulars about the game in question, but I do know I was enthralled. The bell rang for afternoon classes to resume, and everyone else left the auditorium. The game wasn't over, and I stayed. I knew I would get in trouble, but I was too obsessed to let trouble get in my way. I watched until the end, and bravely returned to my classroom. I still recall the odd triumph of that rebellion: I carried feelings of ecstasy over knowing who won and being the only person in the school who had witnessed the victory, but those feelings were juxtaposed with knowing I was about to get into deep trouble with my teacher, Miss Coss, whom I admired and generally tried to please. Perhaps what I learned that day is something that all rebellious spirits learn: It is possible to do the disobedient thing and take great pleasure in it even though there will be unpleasant consequences to endure.

As teenagers, we get better and better at this. (The "we" here is not simply little sisters, needless to say.) As we are less and less under the watchful eyes of adults, we eagerly try out the forbidden fruits of the culture. Even though we know we're not suppose to indulge in any of these things, many of us march right through the list—experimenting with a cigarette, tasting some illegal brew, or seeing if we could get away with attending a forbidden party at a forbidden house for a forbidden amount of time. And, of course, there's sex. Naughty stuff, but naughty in a fairly conventional way. Body adornment, clothing, music, and drugs characterize most adolescent rebellions. Pick any decade. It's entertaining to see how the upcoming generations will express themselves.

In any event, the rebellion that counts, for any particular generation, is the rebellion that turns away from parents' values and thereby exercises independence. Every act we commit that we know they'd disapprove of is surely the stuff of rebellion. Sometimes it feels like some ritual trip through the desert that we have to go on, regardless of the dangers and consequences.

Ursula and her two older sisters, though competitive, were "good," because they sought to fulfill their parents' expectations in both academic and extracurricular activities. Ursula, you may remember, had long hair, which her sisters threatened to cut off in the night. Well, in her mid-teens in the early 1980s, Ursula took it upon herself to undermine their power to threaten her. Those were the early days of punk fashion, and she jumped into the style with both feet. "When I finally got rid of the long hair, I really did it dramatically; I cut it all off except for a tiny braid." She wore all styles of punk hair, including shaving part of her head. She dyed it every color under the rainbow, "except for platinum," she said.

Mischief and rebellion are part of growing up; I doubt many would object to this statement. The degree and types of experiences we engaged in probably depended upon the neighborhoods we lived in, the friends we played with, and, certainly, the siblings we spent so much time with. The shift from mischief to rebellion happened in most of our lives without any realization that such a move was taking place. But some of us did recognize that we'd taken a step we may not have taken at an earlier time. I *knew* that watching the World Series would get me into trouble, but I thought—"It's okay. I'm willing to tolerate the consequences. This moment is worth it to me." Frankly, I felt brave to be putting myself into a risky predicament. Then I put those feelings away and watched the rest of the game. It wasn't until I headed back to my class and found myself walking through empty, quiet halls that my mouth went dry, and I began to fill with dread. Nevertheless, I'd crossed a line that day.

Being rebellious means running a risk, and taking risks is something we last kids are known for. Sometimes we fall flat on our faces, but other times we are able to open doors that lead to places we want to go and to accomplishments we want to achieve, such as making independent decisions about what's important or furthering an important cause in our neighborhood or country. If we use rebellion as an opportunity to shape situations to fit our own desires and creative vision, it can become a valuable tool for advancing our self-esteem and making the world a better place.

Where There's a Will

The will is a wonderful aid to call upon; it leads us to do some bold and remarkable things.

❧

We can't talk about rebellion without talking about will. When we behaved in a manner at odds with what the rest of the family did, we were described as exercising our will. And it was true. Like our emotions, our bodies, and our minds, our wills needed to be exercised in order to fully develop. I believe little sisters focus especially well on developing our will—maybe because we so often see ourselves swimming in the will of others. It is as though we can hear an inner voice: *"We may be little, we may be short, we may not know everything, but if we can activate our will, we can accomplish what we want to do."*

But when we, like our older siblings, exercised that will at age two, we were reined in to meet the family expectations. Many parents hoped that was the end of it, but in some sense it was only the beginning. For those of us with a rebellious spirit, there was no end to our eagerness to exercise our will—it's another way of breathing.

Rebellion is one means that we little sisters use to make ourselves into who we *will* be, and for many of us, it's an ongoing development—continual, if not continuous. The will is a wonderful aid to call upon; it leads us to do some bold and remarkable things. Historically, rebellious little sisters were some of the earliest and most vocal Americans to speak out for the abolition of slavery—Harriet Beecher Stowe's book *Uncle Tom's Cabin* increased the sentiment against slavery, and the Grimké sisters, who had been reared in an aristocratic, southern, slave-holding family, were the first women to speak out publicly against slavery. By their speaking out, these women were rebelling not only against enslavement, but also against the "woman's place," which at the time dictated (through custom and law) that women could not be speakers in public places where both sexes were present.

In recognizing the power of our wills, we can recall that some aspects of it start developing early in our lives. Little kids want and want now. In our teens, a different aspect of will seems to take hold; it is not always predictable, it doesn't always work on our own behalf, and it sometimes spins out of control, but it often gives us the push to rebel. In adulthood, our will becomes more mature. It can still serve our passionate causes, but we can make appropriate use of it. Many of us do.

Our will empowers and activates several aspects of behavior, such as stubbornness, rebellion, and independence. And our will is activated by courage. Courage works better when we have some self-confidence behind it. So there's a long linking of characteristics to inspect. As each aspect takes on a stronger life, the whole chain is improved. We practice using each link: self-confidence, which we exercise among our friends as well as in public arenas of school or work; courage, which is the exercise of self-confidence under adversity; and will, which moves us not to react but to *act* in situations where we believe we must speak up in opposition to authority. For most of us, the development of these abilities grew by incremental steps throughout our childhood and teen years. We felt the urge to take action, and some of us did, while others considered taking action but waited. At some point a moment came when we felt motivated to say "Yes!" to an unpopular idea or an independent action. And our willpower gained full voice.

Proving Ourselves

We engaged in truly rebellious acts, violating written or unwritten rules of behavior, for many reasons.

❧

Louise is in her late forties and is completing her Ph.D. in science education. She had been a teacher for many years before she decided to go to graduate school, which her family saw as disruptive (a symptom of rebelliousness). She readily admits that she is taking a great deal of pride in her accomplishment. She also admits that a good portion of her feelings derive from the fact that she's the little sister in her family; she's proving something she's wanted and needed to prove for a very long time. She feels her family never believed she could earn a Ph.D. It makes the degree that much more precious to her.

Susan followed a fairly typical pattern of youthful rebellion. Her two older brothers set standards of success that left her struggling to keep up. One brother was a whiz in all things academic, and the other was a sports star. No matter what area she pursued, Susan was always compared to her brothers. Instead of enjoying her early years, she said, "I was always having to prove myself."

When she found the path through high school hopelessly strewn with the successes of her brothers, she did a little-sister thing and took a new route. "I was extremely rebellious. I became a terrible student, and I indulged in everything counterculture that I could do without hurting myself."

Her rebelliousness probably helped her sidestep another aspect of sibling comparisons. "There had been a double standard for my brothers and me. When they did bad things, they were often ignored with a comment like, 'Well they're boys.' I was always coming up against that." She escaped those comparisons, perhaps by accident, by not doing the things her brothers did. She may have been doing deeds that her parents strongly objected to, but the opportunity for comparisons vanished. Some people might call little sisters who behave as Susan did "bullheaded." Others may say that her struggles helped her build a strong character. For what it's worth, the result was positive. As an adult, she became co-owner of a very successful company.

We engaged in truly rebellious acts, violating written or unwritten rules of behavior, for many reasons. Sometimes we tried to assert our independence; sometimes we wanted to gain a feeling of camaraderie or love outside of our families; sometimes we wanted to be different—as different as we could be—from our families or the other primary groups we belonged to; and sometimes we wanted to experiment with something we'd never done before. Surely the common activities of rebellion—from dressing unconventionally to talking in code with our friends and seeing movies or reading books we weren't supposed to—were all ways to say "no" to some version of the established culture and "yes" to some version of our own culture.

Postponing the Rebellion

Often we did things that were in opposition to the way the rest of the family lived.

Something to note about rebellion is that it is not always tied to a particular time in life. While the teen years are often pegged as the rebellious years, there are plenty of stories of little sisters who stayed on the "good girl" track through their years in high school. It was only after we left the homestead that we engaged in some of the same rebellious activities—or some new ones—that many of our peers had engaged in earlier.

For those of us who waited to exercise our independence until we were away from home, the rebellion took lots of different paths. Often we did things that were in opposition to the way the rest of the family lived. If we had a solid middle-class upbringing, we might have cut ourselves loose from stability, joined a commune on a Michigan dairy farm, moved to New York City into an apartment with three girls we didn't know, or taken off for a foreign country without any definite plans. Sometimes we've thrown ourselves into whatever counter-culture activities were available at the time. In some instances, we created big successes for ourselves out of something our families didn't understand—like making candles or catering health food to businesses or studying homeopathy or exotic hair braiding. Sometimes getting a degree in philosophy was a rebellious act. Sometimes joining one church or leaving another, or joining a small—or a big—political party represented a huge break with the family traditions. So many ways to rebel.

Glenda found that the conventional path from high school to college provided her with the leverage she needed to engage in her personal rebellion. Having been heavily sheltered through high school, she was eager to go away to college. After doggedly persuading her parents that she'd be okay at a distant school, she succeeded in being allowed to leave her home town. She threw herself into academic life, graduated with honors, and finally established herself in a challenging social work career. Such an exercise of independence was sufficiently rebellious to satisfy Glenda's urges to break away from her family's expectations that she follow a traditional path.

Vanessa performed a more dramatic example of late rebellion. Her outstanding accomplishments in her large Los Angeles high school included distinctions such as being voted Most Likely to Succeed and Most Likely to Be Famous, the Bank of America™ Achievement Award in Fine Arts, Outstanding Student in English, member of the International Society of Thespians, lead actor in her fall drama and spring musical, and serving as a valedictorian of her class, which earned her the opportunity to be one of the speakers before an audience of 5,000 people at graduation. Her father reports that she sent a shock wave through family and friends when they learned that Vanessa and a few other girls celebrated the end of high school by getting their bodies pierced—the day after graduation! Vanessa showed some restraint, according to her dad, in that she selected her tongue as the site for the stud—it can be hidden from public view when she chooses.

While a fairly wide range of rebellion is practiced by little sisters during their early years, it is not uncommon for us to postpone dramatic acts until adulthood. I wonder if we put it off sometimes in order to stay in the good graces of our parents. Maybe we were afraid we'd seriously change the way they felt about us or that we'd make waves in some way that would hurt them. Or if we were in the habit of being good, it may have seemed like too much of a shock to turn into the rascals of all types that we felt like imitating.

Unexpected Turns

Even the little rebellions can surprise the people who thought they knew us so well.

As we little sisters figure out where we want to be when we grow up and make plans to get there, we often move toward a rejection of authority. Sometimes we do it in small ways, and sometimes we make a splash. Even the little rebellions can surprise the people who thought they knew us so well. We little sisters can't rebel without questioning those in charge, which comes to us quite naturally, or disregarding rules from time to time, or simply making decisions that we know will fly in the face of what's expected.

Any look at the lives of many little sisters, both those

who are successful and have made an impact in their field, as well as those of us who lead relatively quiet lives, would reveal more than the usual amount of unexpected turns. Some of the acts are big and noticeable—taking a $3,500 inheritance and buying a plane when you can't fly, as Phoebe Omlie did—and others are smaller moves that simply signify the fact that we're not going to be restricted from exercising our will. In my own case, I think of the no smoking rule in college. My college roommate and I—she a little sister of two brothers and I, of one—scoffed at this rule. Our stance had nothing to do with good or poor health practices; we wanted to smoke because we thought the rule prohibiting it was sanctimonious (and in a rule-riddled campus, it was entertainment to try to get around all regulations). Smoking was not prohibited off campus, of course, but it was strictly forbidden on campus. Administrators wanted to promote a particular image of their students—students who were clean-cut, students who didn't smoke, female students who wore only skirts and dresses, and so on. We wanted to fight it, and so we did.

Maggie and I delighted in busting the no smoking rule in every way possible. We dampened towels to lay across the crack along the bottom of our dorm room door; we exhaled into large plastic bags and then "emptied" the bags out our big window; we taped plastic straws together and draped them over the windowsill, nearly fainting with the energy it took to exhale the smoke down that long and narrow shaft. We even took to smoking pipes for a while in order to replace the distinctive odor of cigarettes with the scent of Cherry Blend™ tobacco. Boy, was it ever fun to purchase pipe tobacco as a college freshman in the sixties! We denied our actions when confronted and thought we were terrifically clever with our sly schemes. And we each lasted less than two years at the school. By choice.

I transferred to the University of Wisconsin, where girls could smoke freely, even in classes, and buy beer in the student union. Wow! My rebellions were so deliciously fostered that I experienced a backlash, dropping out of political science—and its courses filled with tendentious, revolutionary-minded students—and retreated to the safety of linguistics. If acting wild wasn't going to satisfy my rebellious needs, then, like a true exerciser of will, I would find a quietly unconventional major. Oh, the ways of little sisters. We want to keep everyone guessing—including, sometimes, ourselves.

Taking the Risks

✿

Perhaps rebellious acts of little sisters should be viewed as symptoms of growth as we transform from our initial versions into whomever it is we're going to become. Acting rebellious has quite a bit to do with the timing of our lives and a need to exercise independence. Researcher Frank Sulloway claims that we're "unconventional, adventurous, and rebellious," and he ascribes these tendencies to our being more removed from our parents than earlier siblings, so we feel less obliged to align ourselves with their authority. We also feel empathy with the underdogs or those with fewer advantages because of our own histories as last children. Such empathy promotes the likelihood that we'll work for social change, and working for social change means taking risks.[1] If I consider my personal acts of rebellion in light of Sulloway's description, I can take the viewpoint that my semi-surreptitious cigarette smoking in college helped advance personal freedoms.

Some phases of rebellion occur during particular spurts of emotional growth, such as adolescence, being on our own, or perhaps moving to another city. When our spirits are ripe for adventure, rebelliousness is the characteristic that allows us to take opportunities that are unexpectedly available or suddenly appealing to us.

On the other hand, since little sisters have a tendency toward a rebellious nature, satisfying the urge to act up at predictable times in our lives does not mean that it's over. There is every likelihood that we'll also exercise defiance later on, though the inspiration may be vastly different than it was the first time. A person is never too old to join minority causes or leave one job for another or paint a house purple. Some of these acts may be personal whims, but others are worthy on a grand scale and may well enrich the culture, which is a constant need.

Whether rebellions are serious or frivolous, we little sisters are lucky to be endowed with this exceptional inclination. When we feel the urge coming on, we should indulge and enjoy!

For inspiration, consider the little sisters below, whose willingness to go against the grain had an impact on many of our lives:

Adelle Davis—nutritionist

Lorraine Hansberry—playwright, civil rights reformer

Susan Hayward—actor who believed, "It's what you achieve on your own that counts," and shrewdly fought for years to achieve not only popular but artistic success.

Ruth Crawford Seeger—composer, folksinger

Gloria Steinem—outspoken early feminist and a founder of *Ms.* Magazine

Alice B. Toklas—companion and "genius wife" of Gertrude Stein

CHAPTER FIVE

Getting on with Things

*Being female does not constitute the same experience
for a firstborn as it does for a laterborn.*

– FRANK SULLOWAY –

Little sisters deserve a prize for being astonishingly clever.
At different stages of our lives, we encounter all kinds of
predicaments and must figure out how to manage ourselves in each one. We have to assess what's happening
and see if and how we fit in. We have to decide which
tactic to employ in order to gain the best results. As children, we may resort to clever strategies, subtle pressures,
and even physical force—all of which we likely learned
from observing our older brothers or sisters. As we mature, our tools may become more sophisticated versions
of what we did when we were young. Our skills also
expand because we grow, we practice, and we observe.

Little sisters are terrifically keen observers—a result,
I suppose, of our being last and therefore being bound to
do a good deal of watching before we developed our own

modes of expression. Our humble beginnings are a chief reason why little sisters learn about life in a piecemeal way. Of course, everyone learns life tasks bit by bit, but little sisters have so many models to observe and to evaluate that our accumulation of knowledge and experience seems even more deliberate. For some of us, the slow pace is downright painful, but we have little choice. Since most little sisters spend a lot of time *not* being in charge, we have to take our training as we get it. We baby-sit, we take the dog for walks, and we put ice cubes in the drinking glasses before company comes. We busy ourselves watching everyone else manage things, so that by the time we are ready to take over, we've learned a lot. We witness, we watch patiently, we wait for opportunities, and, if need be, we make our own opportunities.

Opportunities to be in charge of various circumstances often seem elusive to us in our early years. When we're children, we may be prevented from being in charge, even though we've heard that our siblings had the same chances when they were our age. We're sometimes babied, which slows down our move into independence whether we like it or not. Eventually, though, most of us find plenty of opportunities to take charge of something—our jobs, our environments, our social situations, our minds.

As we make life-changing decisions, such as finding

a partner or having children, we find ourselves steeped in the activities of adulthood. Throughout those activities we find that we often operate under the influence of our little sister beginnings. Occasionally those leftover effects thwart us to some extent, but more often we find that we can draw strength from the range of experiences and feelings that we enjoyed and endured as little sisters.

Starting Out

We figured out who to please and how to please them so that we could make things happen the way we wanted them to happen.

❦

When we were babies, we acted like babies—taking charge of things and fulfilling our needs by crying or performing other amazing tricks to put ourselves at the center of attention. As we grew and became aware of subtleties, we used our newfound understanding for several purposes: One was to help create a niche for ourselves in the family, and another was to begin to manage whatever was within our territory to manage.

We figured out who to please and how to please them so that we could make things happen the way we wanted them to happen. Sometimes our big brothers and big sisters thought we were giving in when in fact we were plotting. Psychologist Alfred Adler says that we lastborns are more likely to shift ground and to negotiate. Indeed we are. These characteristics are useful in getting what one wants, and we learned them in our homes. This method of being in charge often looked quite conventional. To tell the truth, the fact that we *were* in charge escaped the notice of many of those around us, and sometimes, I'm sorry to report, it even escaped our own attention.

Ellen succeeded in gaining an important role as a child, but she didn't realize how much power she had at her fingertips. She acted as a human "remote control" for the television. At her sister's bidding, Ellen would stand by the television set and change the channels. Meanwhile her big sister reclined on the couch and decided what she wanted to watch. "I don't know why I did it. I just did," Ellen said. Why? Devotion and love, would be my guess. She was certainly accumulating approval points, thereby putting "money in the bank" for the future when she may have wanted something back from big sis.

Getting Respect

Some little sisters find that, regardless of youthful shenanigans, highly respectful relationships with their older siblings can develop in adulthood.

❧

As children, some of us saw obvious ways, such as fighting, to make things work. Susie is a big sister who, when she learned that I was writing this book, sent me a letter with a story about her and her younger sister, Cathy, who died a few years ago. Susie wrote that the sisters had fought mercilessly as kids and that she had enjoyed her status as the older and more powerful sister. One day she egged Cathy on—as usual, she says—and ended the exchange with a punch. Cathy went crying to their father, who, Susie speculated, may have been tired of all the bickering. His advice: "Hit her back." Cathy reentered their shared bedroom and knocked Susie halfway across the room. "After that, our relationship changed," Susie wrote. "Suddenly we were on a level playing field. That was the day we became more than just sisters—we became friends."

It's perhaps dismaying to think that siblings need to come to blows to iron out their frictions, but it's not uncommon. Clearly, it's one way to get on with things. Often a single pop to the arm sent us away from big brother or big sister for the rest of the evening. But the tale of David and Goliath resides in the heart of every little sister who was made to feel physically inferior to her big brother or sister. *Oh, to get one slug in there that will really shock them, really make them understand that you are their equal—if only for a moment.* I guess Susie's dad thought it was time to give a physical confrontation a try, and it worked.

I had a near miss—or a hit and miss—experience in gaining respect that may have put my brother in his place for years. Our family spent a night in a hotel room when I was ten. In the morning, I stayed on my cot the longest, keeping my eyes closed and pretending to be asleep. I thought I heard my parents ask Jerry to wake me, and when I felt someone bend over and kiss me, I shot my fist into the air so fast that bone met cartilage with a smack! A bloody nose! A brief moment of bliss! The bad news was that it wasn't my brother who had planted the kiss, but my father. Horrors! Fortunately for me, my dad has a good sense of humor, so he thought the event was funny, even as his nose bled and bled. I was never able to give my brother such a successful punch, but I wonder if the clocking I gave my dad also gave pause to my brother. We were near the end of punching games, and perhaps my misplaced pop sped that process.

Some little sisters find that, regardless of youthful shenanigans, highly respectful relationships with their older siblings can develop in adulthood. Sarah, who wasn't particularly close to her older brother in childhood, found a new bond with him after they'd grown. Perhaps, she says, it was "because I lost my father just as I was entering adulthood and always felt the need for older, masculine, fatherly energy in my life. We began to spend more and more time together, and even though we now live on opposite coasts, I try to see him annually.

"A couple of years ago we decided to take a wilderness camping trip together. My brother spent a good deal of time researching where and when to go, what the costs would be, and what to expect on the trip. It had been many years since I had done a wilderness trip, and the same was true for my brother. But there we were—two middle-aged people, with all our gear, one map, a canoe, and a pack of food.

"After driving down a dusty old gravel road for hours, our outfitter dropped us off in a swamp. We were to canoe thirty-five miles, through a series of lakes and portages, to the leeward shore of a lake deep in the wilderness where a seaplane would pick us up four days later.

"We 'put in,' and I looked at the map and panicked. I couldn't imagine how we could find our way to our end point with that map—the amount of detail was meager. Translating the vastness of the Canadian wilderness to a rendering of that scale seemed impossible to me. But my brother, completely nonplussed by the situation, immediately took charge and started navigating.

"We got lost our second day on the trail, but eventually he found our way. Then we ran into horrible weather—rain, thunder, lightning. One night several storms accompanied by high winds and cold came roaring through. My tent started to leak, I hadn't had dinner because of the torrential downpour, and I had worked hard all day. I lay in my tent whimpering, worried that we would never leave the island on which we were camping, that we would never make it to our pickup point in time, and that the outfitter would never find us again.

"My brother called from his tent, saying not to worry, and to try to sleep. The next day it was still raining, but not as hard, and we took off. Finally the skies cleared, and he and I had a great discussion about fear, risks, taking chances, and the importance of finding your own way. I learned so much from him about myself. And I was so touched that he was willing to talk about such personal issues with me. I'll never forget that trip."

Sarah's experience with her brother conveyed one of those rare events where adult siblings share a major experience that nurtures their relationship. One result of the camping trip seems to have been a leap forward in the mutual respect that the two already held for one another.

As children, siblings aren't capable of the subtleties of language that helped Sarah and her brother articulate their emotions. In childhood, we often express ourselves physically to gain the respect that we want: a won race or a thrown punch. All kinds of things can contribute to that virtue that we little sisters long for so dearly—respect.

The Little Princess

Even if we little sisters grow up enough to want an end to special treatment and even if we actually develop into strong and independent young women, our history can continue to invade our lives.

❧

Sometimes one of the phases that little sisters experience is an extended infancy. Being coddled is fine for babies, but it doesn't suit most of us beyond that phase. A study by psychologist J. K. Lasko indicated that youngest girls are often babied beyond babyhood and that second children (who are often the youngest) are pampered and protected more in their preschool years than first children.[1] The finding contradicts the conventional notion that new parents are more nervous and more conscientious about protecting their first child, while they lighten up on the second. (Indeed, several little sisters reported feeling lucky to be spared the strict parenting their older siblings endured during their teen years.)

On the other hand, a little sister in the house provides the perfect excuse for older siblings to behave like miniature grown-ups. The ideal way for older siblings— even the still young ones—to exercise their new maturity is to protect and pamper the newest member of the family. As parents see their older children moving into more peer experiences, it may be a perfectly natural thing for them to baby the youngest as one way to hold onto that idyllic phase of early parenthood. For us, it's not perfectly natural; instead, it feels like excessive clinging, and most of us are willing, if not eager, to abandon it.

Even if we little sisters grow up enough to want an end to special treatment and even if we actually develop into strong and independent young women, our history can continue to invade our lives. Hillary, the youngest of four girls, received the reputation of being the princess in the family. Her sisters undoubtedly witnessed and probably helped eagerly with her early coddling. A few decades later, though, despite her various acts of rebellion and living an independent life, her three older sisters still pull out the "princess" tag when they want to avoid dealing with hard issues. Such an avoidance strategy is a way of maintaining control or a way of making sure that we little sisters don't get to take charge.

By contrast, sometimes behaving like a princess is a way to exercise independence. Ruth remembers when one of her three older brothers was selling popcorn from a stand on the street during a town celebration. She asked him for some, assuming that since he was her brother, he'd give her a bag. Instead, he said, "Hold out your hands." He gave her the amount that would fit into her small, cupped hands, and she was so insulted that she dropped her hands and let the popcorn fall to the ground. *Nothing* was better than *not enough*.

In childhood, Katherine enjoyed a privilege that is perhaps granted only to siblings close in age, and, even then, it's rare. Katherine says she did lots of things at a younger age "than I would have if I hadn't had an older sister. It was like, we were both girls, and we were close in age, so if Barb got to do something, I'd get to tag along and do it, too."

Patricia also enjoyed such a privilege. Each time her

sister, who was twenty-two months older, gained another foothold in adulthood—staying up a little later, going somewhere without parental supervision—Patricia was granted the perk at the same time. What a powerful way to undercut the gloating of older siblings.

I wonder if our older siblings sometimes watched us being pampered and getting early privileges, and interpreted the treatment as our being spoiled. For us, who were in the middle of that experience, the truth was often *not* that we felt spoiled, but that we felt constrained. Early privileges did not necessarily translate into mature treatment. Therefore, if we took our experiential learning to heart and acted like a princess sometimes, I suspect we believed such action was among our choices of how to react as we moved along the path to independence. The fact is that there may have been moments in our lives when grasping power with a royal flair may have been the only way that we could exercise authority.

Going Home Again

Sometimes when we go home, we find that older sibs treat us as an equal—and we suddenly realize that we no longer need to hope for this occurrence.

❧

An inescapable phenomenon occurs for most of us little sisters after we discover what it feels like to be in charge for some period of time in the world outside of our own families. We may feel that we've done a good job of getting on with our lives, and then we go home—the home that's built of siblings and parents. Sometimes the clock turns back and we become the little sisters that we were as young kids. Alas. Our powers shrivel or at least shift around while we are with our family and stay that way until we can return to our own turf.

This difference between a person's behavior at home and her or his behavior in society has recently become more widely recognized. Judith Rich Harris, author of *The Nurture Assumption,* argues that, besides the genetic influence, character and personality are shaped by peers and not parents. I certainly believe that *behavior* is acutely influenced by peers, but I also believe that our early years in the family have a profound effect on who we are.

Along with her controversial belief in the power of peers, Harris recognizes that birth order has influence within the family structure. "If you see people with their parents or their siblings you do see the differences you expect to see. The oldest does seem more serious, responsible, and bossy. The youngest does behave in a more carefree fashion." But studies show that people often behave quite differently when they're away from their families and on their own.[2]

Little sisters are aware of that difference, but there can occasionally be an unexpected turn of events, even at the homestead. Sometimes when we go home, we find that older sibs treat us as an equal—and we suddenly realize that we no longer need to hope for this occurrence. I remember feeling several steps behind my brother when our adult families gathered. He always seemed to have read *The Wall Street Journal* cover to cover, to be up on the latest developments in national and international politics, and to know just a whole lot of other hot news. How could I ever keep up? But then came the first visit after we'd both purchased computers. I could suddenly talk megabytes, RAM, DOS versions, icons, and virus control. The conversation made me feel as if we'd entered an entirely new era.

Sarah also describes a relationship with her big brother

that developed into something very satisfying. "Today, as adults, our relationship is still that of big brother/little sister, although he is very respectful of me and my accomplishments. Sometimes when I have a big decision to make and need someone like-minded to mull it over with, I call my brother. He is always helpful, cheerful, and best yet, has similar values to mine so I don't have to explain my way of thinking or how I feel."

We little sisters are very transparent in our desires. It's simple. We'd like to return to our homes and enjoy the same kind of dignified respect that we receive in our own worlds. I guess it's a lot to ask, but perhaps little sisters as parents can remember to make a note of this desire and tuck it into their last daughter's baby book as a reminder of what might be called the golden rule of parenting—doing unto our children as we would have liked our families to do unto us.

Pairing and Parenting

The challenge, it seems, is to recognize when we're relying on our childhood dynamics.

❧

Because we can see so many ways in which being a little sister affects our lives, we can't be too surprised to discover that our birth placement may affect the kind of people we attach ourselves to. Some studies have found that our birth order not only influences our choice in a mate, but also how well things work out, depending on the birth order match.

Researcher Walter Toman found that oldest brothers and youngest sisters often become partners, as do youngest brothers and oldest sisters.[3] Such marriages do fairly well, he found, because often the specific sibling pattern is mirrored—a little sister with an older brother marries a man who is an older brother of a little sister. Troublesome, or at least challenging, are marriages between two firstborns—"who's in charge" can become a continuing theme—and two lastborns, who'd both like to kick back and have the other person run things.[4]

I confess that I fit quite neatly into Toman's statistics. I can have rollicking good fun with middle or youngest brothers, but with few exceptions, I'm seriously attracted only to oldest brothers or only children. I wonder if I've repeated this model with my husband because I know the sibling games—the teasing, the joking around—and I have the expectation that he'll get bossy once in a while because he grew up with that privilege. I also know that he won't be surprised when I throw his bossiness right back at him; after all, I'm now a *grown-up* little sister, and I don't need to put up with such behavior any longer. (It usually works.) Fortunately, we also operate with a large dose of humor.

One little sister says, "I find that a lot of the men whom I am attracted to as an adult resemble my brother in one way or another. My sister-in-law laughs whenever I start talking about a new boyfriend, because the description often starts with 'Well, he sort of reminds me of my brother . . .'"

Mimi, too, finds that she weighs a new love on how well he matches up to her older brother. "The way my older brother treats me is my standard for how I want to be treated in a relationship. He's kind; he's concerned about my life; he listens when I talk about how I feel; he's loyal; he'd bash someone's head in if they tried to hurt me. Well, he wouldn't actually do it, but I love it when he says he would. This is the kind of respect I want from a man."

Not all younger siblings find that the younger/older matchup works for them. Researcher Lucille Forer cited a little sister and lastborn male who continually partnered with people who were firstborns. In each case, the younger sibling repeated their childhood pattern: complete dependence, development of some independence, accusations against the partner for being bossy, hurt feelings, and, finally, splitting up.[5] The challenge, it seems, is to recognize when we're relying on our childhood dynamics. Sometimes they may suit the situation perfectly (whining, bossing, teasing, flattery) and other times they're inappropriate.

So while grown-up siblings may still understand how to behave like a big brother or a little sister, mature adults also know that there's another level of behavior. We recognize childhood patterns in some of our feelings and dealings with people, and we find ourselves acquiring new, mature methods of relating to people. It's useful to have the full panorama of behaviors at our fingertips because life is full of surprises, and one may need all acceptable tactics at one time or another. (We probably want to abandon pinching and pouting in most situations, though I'm sure any of us could imagine some scene where these strategies might be useful.) The point is, again, that in order to assure a promotion or to deflate a testy moment, we little sisters (and some of our siblings) are always up for finding ways to improve ourselves and develop new behaviors, even while we cherish the old ones.

As we have learned about the ways we match up with partners and how those matches work, we must also look at the other matches of our lives: the children. What happens when little sisters become mothers? Being a parent is the ultimate opportunity to take charge and to exercise a slew of strategies. It's an exercise in constant decision making while aiming to have the best-behaved and happiest kids in the universe.

It turns out that research is on our side when it comes to our parenting skills. We lastborn children have lucky kids. Apparently we may not be enthusiastic about the idea of becoming parents, but when we do so, we are playful and helpful. We're also kind and gentle, so we're especially helpful to the weakest children (and we know that for a time, the youngest is the weakest). We're also vivacious and spontaneous, which tends to make a fun home.[6] On the down side, we can also be overprotective since we were overprotected as children. I'd argue that if we remember how much we hated being overprotected, we probably will parent differently—maybe even granting too much independence too early!

Other findings about parental behavior based on parents' birth order indicates that oldest sisters tend to continue with the overachieving drive, middle sisters' behavior is varied and depends upon whom they marry, and little sisters can also assume differing parenting behaviors depending upon partners—we lastborn-sisters-turned-parents also often vacillate between being indulgent and stern.[7] We can each point to pieces of our history that lead us to behave in some of the ways we do as parents. We try, and we try. There's no end to learning.

Astute Observers

As small people, we little sisters didn't have to give this behavior a second thought; watching others was an important survival tactic.

Whoever coined the phrase:"Knowledge is power" was probably either a little sister or had one.

We little sisters know lots of things from our years of observing the family. While we were busy making a place for ourselves, we had something else going on. The something else was an acute awareness of everyone around us and how they were reacting and interacting. We watched and listened, and we tried to make sense of the give and take, of the joy and jest, of the tease and touch.

When I visualize this concept, I think of a pointillist's painting, and I realize what a challenging undertaking all this observation is for young little sisters. Consider *Sunday in the Park* by George Seurat or any of Monet's gardens or Chuck Close's portraits. To stand within inches of these paintings is to see dots. Lovely, colorful dots. Each step back adds more, dots of different colors and dots that are closer or farther apart. The astute viewer begins to see the dots take on shapes as a unit. Suddenly, a unit becomes a very identifiable figure.

So it is with little sisters. We see the dots of behavior, and we try to figure out what's good and what's bad. At first, we see the tiniest of details, but as we grow, the opportunities to observe multiply, and we gain experience in watching the picture of our family interactions expand. As it expands, the dots begin to fall together into outlines and shapes, and we gain wisdom about the dynamics of our family.

As small people, we little sisters didn't have to give this behavior a second thought; watching others was an important survival tactic. This action is a useful one; it leads us to be highly astute observers and sensitive beings, and it helps us understand not only how to take charge and get on with things, but also when the time is right to do so.

We might think of two types of knowledge here. One is the knowledge we need to get through life—how to interact with people, how to use our creativity, how to manage resources, how to laugh and love—and the other is the knowledge of our civilization.

Lynda is a little sister who gained a lot of knowledge that contributed to her self-respect as well as a lifelong interest in education. She was exposed to very sophisticated ideas at a very young age. Her sister and brother, eleven and twelve years older, left for college the years that Lynda was four and five. Education was emphasized strongly in her home, and when her siblings returned from college, they were eager to share what they'd learned. Her sister read a lot of poetry to her, and her brother read her novels. By age fourteen she was familiar with many great poets and had read authors that few junior high students tackle. Some of the writers were Andre Malreaux, Saul Bellow, and Albert Camus. Lynda also says that her siblings instilled in her an optimism from the 1960s. "What my siblings did were real gifts to me," she says.

Angela, too, found her older brother to be a source of knowledge. He was in his second year of college when

Angela entered high school. "I adored him. He was a good student and very intellectually curious. I used to spend hours in his room (when he wasn't there) reading his books. I discovered Charles Dickens that way and T. S. Eliot. He would bring home music from college: Stan Getz, Buffy Saint Marie, Joan Baez, The Beatles, and many more interesting people. He even taught me to play chess."

Sometimes, learning a lot can make a big impression at school, work, or in the public eye. As a reminder of little sisters who have used their knowledge to advance civilization, here are a few names you probably recognize:

Virginia Apgar—physician who developed infant rating scale

Rachel Carson—conservationist writer

Anita Hill—law professor who spoke out against the confirmation of Clarence Thomas to the Supreme Court

Karen Horney—psychoanalyst who disagreed strongly with Sigmund Freud

Blanche Wolf Knopf—editor, publisher

Marianne Moore—poet and critic

Dorothy Parker—writer and social wit

And there are many who've made their mark with less public attention in virtually every field—from laboratory research, education, and religion to astronomy, computer science, and the arts.

Telling All

From tattling to memoirs, our desire to tell secrets and reveal family stories carries over into adulthood.

❦

It happens that we little sisters are not known for our ability to keep secrets. Sometimes, though, we hold out just long enough to assert a smidgen of power; it's very satisfying. The fact is that we believe in, and value, telling. It's a powerful thing to do. From tattling to memoirs, our desire to tell secrets and reveal family stories carries over into adulthood.

Ursula told me that she was surprised to realize that she, and not her two older sisters, is the one interested in spending time in Germany to learn more about their family history. All of them had lived there as children, but she's the one who is eager to go back and explore her roots more thoroughly. She added, "I'm also the one who's more open with emotions and other things. I'm much more likely to reveal both feelings and experiences to others; I've been called to the carpet for it, but I just don't see that it's wrong."

It's generally the youngest who tends to write the family histories and the tell-all autobiographies. Apparently, we don't particularly value the code of keeping the closet door closed. (Sorry, Jerry, Mom, and Dad. I can't help it. I *am* the little sister.)

The Desire to Do Well

But then an opportunity arose where
I could test my skills.

Sometimes we little sisters seek a golden moment of promise and pride in the family circle. When it works, it's grand, when it flops, we add another badge to our banner of "lessons learned."

When I was on the brink of adulthood in the mid-1960s, our family took a whirlwind trip to Europe—seven countries in three weeks. We'd never been, and I guess we thought we'd never go again, so my parents packed it as full as they could.

My mother spoke Norwegian and would take care of us in Oslo, my brother spoke German and would field the questions in several German cities, and I'd studied

French, so I was expected to take charge of communication for our three days in that country. (My dad liked to add that since he spoke English, he'd take care of us in London.)

As it turned out, we found English speakers in France nearly everywhere we turned, which was good because the speed at which the native tongues flew seemed to have little to do with the subject matter or style of my school-room French ("I now enter the classroom." "Do you have a hat?" "I see your nose"). But then an opportunity arose where I could test my skills. We ran out of clean clothes and wanted to wash them. We kept a lookout for a self-service laundry, but with no luck. So finally our entire family marched into a small, dark, professional clothes cleaning establishment so that I could ask the location of such a place. I had my dictionary, which had no direct translation of the words, but I constructed what seemed like an able French description. Family members looked on as I struggled to ask the three workers about a place to wash one's own clothes—with the key verbs and pronouns in place—and their only response was a lot of slow shaking of the head. Bafflement. My humiliation ran deep. Any authority and respect I'd expected to gain by virtue of my specialized knowledge was kaput. Oh, to lose such an opportunity.

Years later, I learned that laundries with self-service washing didn't exist in Paris in those days. But the knowledge came too late to save the face I'd lost that day.

Staying in Touch

This geographical spreading out that so many of us do was mentioned by several little sisters as a reason for not being as close to their siblings as they might be.

❧

We little sisters end up with a whole range of relationships with our siblings once we're all grown. Some couldn't be closer (Maeve and her sister recently took a vacation together), and others find that they have little in common (Laura and Diana live hundreds of miles away from their big sisters, and they allow the geography to keep them apart socially and emotionally, too).

In my own case, my brother and I feel a closeness, but at the same time we comfortably go months between telephone calls. I think our adult relationship is similar to what it was when we were kids. We weren't great buddies, but we knew we could talk to each other when we wanted.

Except for a brief time in our elementary school

years, I was always in a different school than he was. Once he'd gone off to college, he spent his summers working on the East Coast, and then I moved to the West Coast. I don't recall in those years that we ever went out for a coffee or a beer. But he certainly saved my life when I was three (the water pump on the farm), and he has come to my rescue since. Some years ago, I had left a bad situation and was newly living on my own, hand-to-mouth, with a part-time teaching job that paid for about three-quarters of a month's cost of living. He had no idea how tight things were, since it wasn't the kind of thing I would tell him. But I had a great shock one day near the penny-pinching end of the month, when I opened a letter from him and found a kind note and a check for $200. It was a true lifeline for which I will be forever grateful.

He has always been concerned about my life and my activities—even when he was as much of a Republican as he could be and I was as much of a Democrat as I could be. He's gone out of his way to pay me visits now and again, too. I suspect there's a bit of the protective older brother still active there. I haven't felt censure from him, even when I've done some pretty ridiculous things. If we lived in the same city, I know we'd spend more time together. This geographical spreading out that so many of us do was mentioned by several little sisters as a reason for not being as close to their siblings as they might be.

The converse of this can be true, too. Doris and her three older sisters live within two hundred miles of one another. They come together annually for what they call "Sisters' Day." The custom has gone on for fifteen years, and the year that the oldest sister, who was eighty, lost her husband, the women decided to spend the entire weekend together to have plenty of time to talk, shop, eat, and do some sightseeing in the small town where they grew up. It was a good time for sisterly support, too.

Doris said that when the four of them were young, there were typical squabbles; however, the eighteen-year spread between the oldest and the youngest softened some of the difficult times. The four of them are very close now.

And for many little sisters, geography isn't a deterrent to emotional closeness. Margaret and her sister—three years older—enjoyed a mostly tranquil childhood on a farm. They played with paperdolls—the clothing models cut from the Montgomery Ward and Sears and Roebuck catalogs. "We helped each other with our scrapbooks, too," Margaret recalls. She collected articles about the Dionne quintuplets. The sisters helped their mother in the garden and sometimes were allowed to bring a kitten inside to play, where they would dress the little creature in doll clothes and push it around in a buggy. Margaret adds, "When you put a bonnet and dress on a kitten, it will do just about anything you want it to." She admired her sister when they were young, and despite the hundreds of miles between them all through their adulthood, the two have always been close.

If little sisters develop an emotional closeness with their older brothers and sisters when they're young and nurture it into adulthood, it seems that no amount of distance can keep them from maintaining their relationship. On the other hand, if the siblings don't want to be dependent upon each other or share the experiences of their lives, no amount of technology in the way of telephones, the U.S. Post Office, or even e-mail can force them into being close. Life changes, however, can sometimes force the issue. Regardless, there are lots of answers to the question of what it means to be close.

When Misfortunes Happen

If any sibling asks for help, the door opens for a relationship that may be far different from anything previously practiced.

❦

Sometimes we're brought together through inevitable misfortunes that occur. No family is without bad times. Illness and death, accidents or downsizing, floods or drugs. For many families, these hard times provide, for the first time in years, a chance for personal conversations. If any sibling asks for help, the door opens for a relationship that may be far different from anything previously practiced. A favor offered, a crisis to deal with, thanks given. All of these moments may be unusual in the life we're accustomed to, and each of them presents an opportunity for a different type of response—or more responses—than the routine ones that have been part of the exchanges we've had over the years.

One such situation occurred with Karen. Karen said that she and her brother, who is thirteen years older and lived several hours away, were close in some ways but didn't have a lot of contact. As they took care of their aging parents, they started communicating more regularly. When their father died recently, both children were able to be with him when he passed away. The bond "drew us closer together again," she says.

As well as having a chance to grow closer to older siblings, little sisters find that a family crisis may suddenly demand that they assume a role of leadership and become the caretakers when family members fall ill or have other troubled times. Women, more than men, fulfill this role of caretaking, but among my friends, I've seen little sisters carry the burden more often than children in other birth positions.

Regardless of the events and complex relationships within our families, it is probably true that taking charge of our lives is something that happens outside of the family a great deal more often than it happens within those long-held boundaries. Opportunities for being competent in our jobs or social organizations or in our homes—whether our family consists of one beloved pet or if we live with a blended family numbering seven or more—grow steadily in our adult years. Many of the roles we play in both our public and private lives provide us with the chance to call upon the rich background that we carry from our lives as little sisters. It can be deeply gratifying to have our resources valued by family members in a family crisis. It may feel like a big, "Finally!"

Growing into Our Shoes

Because little sisters spend so many weeks and months and years being bossed, I suspect that when the moment comes that we find we're in charge of something big at home (driving to the store for milk or being unexpectedly in charge of grilling the burgers), we're taken by surprise. Even when we suddenly have authority in our public lives, many of us find we need time to grow into it.

To have people address us as specialists in some area undoubtedly feels good, but it can take some getting used to. I heard a story of a little sister who earned a Ph.D. in anthropology. When she walked across the stage to receive her diploma and heard the words that described her, she looked around, expecting that someone else was the recipient of the honor.

Another little sister, Patricia, realized when she was in graduate school that she had finally gained a sense of being free to do what she wanted to do. Yet she believes that her years of continuing education also represented a way to postpone adult responsibilities. Postponed, perhaps, but not permanently avoided. Patricia now holds a prestigious management position.

As adults, we little sisters have a wonderful array of characteristics to draw from. Our struggles with being the smallest child taught us doggedness and perseverance in the face of trying to keep up with our siblings. When our siblings invited us to participate in their mischief, we learned about cooperation (we already knew how to take orders) and about how to get into and out of trouble. We often worked hard to compete with our siblings, which may have meant excelling in a field they had never been involved in. And some of us felt the fiercest loyalty and friendships with our own sisters and brothers. Our lives at home taught us adaptability and friendliness, which led to our being popular.[8] We have abilities that help us get along well with partners and in the work place. And our kids think we're fun.

We sometimes felt so protected and sheltered that we took risks that—surprise!—people thought were out of character for us. Other times we took off on adventures of the mind, spirit, or body, just to enjoy the feeling of independence and self-control. In many ways being born last helped us appreciate others who were in the underdog position, which makes us eager to work on social change, no matter what the risk, and also contributes to our being kind parents. As we grew and developed into adults, we became aware that we had a lot to offer.

The success of our pursuits lent us the confidence and self-esteem to move forward into new challenges. Over time, as we pull these attributes together and understand their roots, we realize that our life as a little sister is an unmistakable asset.

Little sisters work hard to achieve both small and extraordinary successes, and we take pride in our accomplishments. Every inch of the way, we carry along a history that reminds us of what it was like to be the littlest and the last. Meanwhile, each of us opens ourselves to adventure and possibility, again and again. The perspective we enjoy throughout our lives, regardless of whether we were one of the pampered ones or one of the strugglers, gives us a rich human experience that, in the end, makes us pleased to be one of the women in the world who can say, "I'm a little sister."

Endnotes

CHAPTER ONE

1. Heinz L. Ansbacher and Rowena R. Ansbacher, *The Individual Psychology of Alfred Adler* (New York: Harper Torchbooks, 1956), 376.
2. Brian Sutton-Smith and B. G. Rosenberg, *The Sibling* (New York: Holt, Rinehart and Winston, Inc., 1970), 40-45.

3. Ibid., 27-29.

4. Ibid., 40-45.

5. Walter Toman, *Family Constellation: Its Effects on Personality and Social Behavior,* 4th ed. (New York: Springer Publishing Company, 1993), 178-180.

6. R. R. Sears, E. E. Maccoby, and H. Levin, *Patterns of Child Rearing* (Evanston, Illinois: Row, Peterson & Co., 1957), quoted in John A. Clausen, Francena Hancock, Judith Williams, Katherine Jako, *Family Size and Birth Order as Influences Upon Socialization and Personality* (Berkeley: University of California, Social Science Research Council, Committee on Socialization and Social Structure, 1965), 136.

7. Lucille K. Forer with Henry Still, *The Birth Order Factor* (New York: David McKay Company, Inc., 1976), 222.

8. J. W. Macfarlane, L. Allen, and M. P. Honzik, *A Developmental Study of the Behavior Problems of Normal Children between 21 Months and 14 Years* (Berkeley: University of California Publication in Child Development, University of California Press, 1954), quoted in Clausen et al., *Family Size and Birth Order,* 105-106.

9. Ibid., 106.

10. Forer, *Birth Order Factor,* 128-131.

11. Toman, *Family Constellation,* 171.

12. Forer, *Birth Order Factor,* 132-133.

13. Ibid., 133-134.

14. Ibid., 128.

15. Ibid., 135-136.

16. Encyclopedia Britannica Online (Chicago: Britannica Centre, 1998).

CHAPTER TWO

1. Forer, *Birth Order Factor,* 93.

2. J. H. S. Bossard, "Family Modes of Expression," *American Sociological Review* 10 (1945): 226-237, quoted in Clausen et al., *Family Size and Birth Order,* 32.

3. Encyclopedia Britannica Online, entry on Eric Heiden.

4. Forer, *Birth Order Factor,* 110.

5. Gene Slack Scharlau, *Notable American Women: The Modern Period* eds. Barbara Sicherman, Carol Hurd Green (Cambridge, Mass.: The Belknap Press of Harvard University Press, 1980), 515-517.

6. I. D. Harris, *The Promised Seed: A Comparative Study of Eminent First and Later Sons* (New York: The Free Press of Glencoe, 1964), quoted in Clausen et al., *Family Size and Birth Order,* 74-75.

7. Toman, *Family Constellation,* 177-178.

8. Forer, *Birth Order Factor,* 133-134.

9. Ibid., 102.

10. Ibid.

11. Ibid., 244.

12. Frank J. Sulloway, *Born to Rebel: Birth Order, Family*

Dynamics, and Creative Lives (New York: Pantheon Books, 1996), 85.

CHAPTER THREE

1. Sulloway, *Born to Rebel,* 98.
2. Ibid., xiv.
3. Ibid., 77.
4. Sutton-Smith, *The Sibling,* 25.
5. Ibid., 26.
6. Ibid., 25.
7. Sulloway, *Born to Rebel,* 110.

CHAPTER FOUR

1. Sulloway, *Born to Rebel,* 70.

CHAPTER FIVE

1. J. K. Lasko, "Parent Behavior Toward First and Second Children," *Genetic Psychology Monographs* 49 (1954): 96–137, quoted in Clausen et al., *Family Size and Birth Order,* 96–100.
2. Judith Rich Harris, *The Nurture Assumption: Why Children Turn Out the Way They Do* (New York: The Free Press, 1998), 61.
3. Walter Toman, cited in Forer, *Birth Order Factor,* 185.
4. Walter Toman, cited in Sutton-Smith, *The Sibling,* 7.
5. Forer, *Birth Order Factor,* 185.
6. Ibid., 217.
7. Ibid., 218–220.
8. Sutton-Smith, *The Sibling,* 117.

Acknowledgments

I want to express my gratitude to the little sisters who so generously shared their funny, touching, irksome, difficult, triumphant stories with me; some names in the manuscript have been changed at their request.

I also want to acknowledge the tireless assistance and good spirits of the cast and crew at Circulus Publishing Group, Inc./Wildcat Canyon Press—Roy M. Carlisle, my editor, for his support and guidance; Julienne Bennett, my publisher, for her passion for the subject; Tamara Traeder, for her support and thoughts on being a little sister; Holly A. Taines, for her meticulous care in processing the manuscript and the proofs; Rose Bargmann, for her sales and marketing support; and the rest of the staff for their help in sundry ways.

Finally, I want to give public acknowledgment for the support of my family—Craig, Adria, Rachel, and Given—most of whom enjoy reminding me that they're firstborn, but who all nevertheless offered encouragement and patience, along with the occasional dumb joke.

About the Author

Carolyn Lieberg earned degrees in Linguistics and Non-Fiction Writing from the University of Wisconsin at Madison and the University of Iowa, respectively. She has served as editor of *Iowa Woman* and for the Carnegie Foundation for the Advancement of Teaching, and is now Associate Director for the Center for Teaching at the University of Iowa.

Carolyn was born in Watertown, South Dakota. Today she lives in Iowa City, Iowa—just hours away from her still older, and still bigger, brother—with her husband and stepson.

❧

Wildcat Canyon Press publishes books that embrace such subjects as friendship, spirituality, women's issues, and home and family, all with a focus on self-help and personal growth. Great care is taken to create books that inspire reflection and improve the quality of our lives. Our books invite sharing and are frequently given as gifts.

For a catalog of our publications, please write:

WILDCAT CANYON PRESS
2716 Ninth Street, Berkeley, California 94710
Phone: (510) 848-3600
Fax: (510) 848-1326
Circulus@aol.com